THE AMERICAN HOUSE

DESIGN FOR LIVING

VOLUME ONE

THE AMERICAN HOUSE

DESIGN FOR LIVING

The American Institute of Architects Press,
Washington, D.C.

and

The Images Publishing Group,
Melbourne, Australia

THE AMERICAN INSTITUTE OF ARCHITECTS HOUSING COMMITTEE

Richard H. Bradfield, FAIA, Chair

Bruce Downing, AIA, Vice Chair

Philip S. Handler, AIA

John V. Mutlow, AIA

Britten L. Perkins, AIA

William E. Pelham, AIA, Commissioner

Patrick J. Lally, Staff Director

Published jointly by
The American Institute of Architects Press
1735 New York Avenue, NW
Washington, DC 20006

and

The Images Publishing Group
"Images House"
6 Bastow Place
Mulgrave, Victoria 3170
Australia

© 1992 The American Institute of Architects
All rights reserved

Library of Congress Cataloging-in-Publication Data

The American house: design for living/edited by John V. Mutlow.

    p. cm.

  Includes index.

    ISBN 1-55835-027-6 USA   ISBN 1 875498 10 9 Australia

    1. Architecture, Domestic–United States–Designs and plans.

  I. Mutlow, John V.

  NA7205.A66 1992

  728'.022'273–dc20   91-39682

                                      CIP

Contents

Foreword　初めに	7
Preface　序文	9
The Custom Single-Family Home　一世帯注文住宅	11
Production and Semi-Custom Housing　建売・半注文住宅	51
Multi-Family Housing　多世帯住宅	71
Community and Master Plan Housing　総合都市計画	111
Index　インデックス	129

初めに

言うまでもないことであるが、住宅の未来は、単に分譲と造成だけでなく地域や町を創り出せるかどうかという点にかかっている。現在、住宅建設の場所というものは主に3つを数える。一つは中心都市、次第に乱れている伝統的な近郊地域、いわば「中間都市」、そして残された最も美しい景観に余りに多くの事が余りに急速に起こっている辺境地域、である。

それぞれの場所に単に異なる住宅が必要となるだけでなく、それぞれに見合った土地管理と場所作りが必要とされるわけである。中心都市においては、50年に亘る再開発の努力の殆どが惨めな失敗に終わっているため、何らかの道を模索しなければならない。人々のための公共道路を取り戻し、私邸のファサードを寄せ集めただけでなく、全体で公共の風景となるような壁の形態を開発することが必要となる。中間都市においては、第二次世界大戦以前の都市計画モデルを再検討することから始めなければならない。そのいわゆる路面電車的近郊地域は、都市の交通網に組み込まれているが、都市とは異なる近隣地域としての個性を確固として保持し、非常に住みやすくそして時に芸術的とも言える要素を作り出していた。私個人はボストン郊外のブルックライン、フィラデルフィアのチェスナット・ヒルそしてニューヨーク・クイーンズのサニーサイドをイメージしている。

更にその外側の地域においては、古くからの分譲の状況は記録に残っているが、私達は更に土地を侵食し、つまらぬどこともないような場所を生み続けている。一体、私達の都市はどこまで広がるのであろうか？都市計画が一つの統一体となるのを止め、何もない中心を持つドーナツ型に近似して行くまでに、一体どれだけの事をとらえることができるのであろうか？

二人用のワールプールバスや3台収納のガレージが家庭的な家屋設備に取って代わってしまう時代においては、住宅のデザインについて楽観視することは難しい。物質的な安楽は増進しているだろうが、建築が日常生活のドラマの舞台セットするものであるのならば、そのドラマは舞台を遥かに逸脱してしまった。本書に収録したプロジェクトが、良い建築というものは単なる雨よけを特別なものへと昇華させる力を持つという事を示していても、ページ上に紹介できるものは現在造られているもののほんの僅かの部分に過ぎない。そして現在アメリカで造られている大量の住宅はかなり興味をそそるものなのである。しかし最良の作品といえども十分とはいえない。そこに住むにしろ働くにしろ、人々が集まる場所で必要とされるものというのは個々の作品のデザインの改良というレベルでは満たせないものである。真に必要なことは住宅建築というのは環境的文化的行為なのであるという新しい理解である。

建築家として、私達は過去に造られたものの最良のものを知る義務がある。そして過去の業績に少なくとも並ぶようにしなければならない。そして何よりも私達は日常生活環境から芸術を造り出す責任を負っているのである。

1991年11月

ロバート・A.M.・スターン

Foreword

It is a truism that the future of housing depends on whether we can succeed in creating neighborhoods and towns and not merely developments and subdivisions. There are three principal locales for building housing today: the center city; the "middle city" – that is, the increasingly troubled old line suburbs; and the fringes, where too much is happening too fast to some of the most beautiful landscape that remains to us.

Each locale calls not just for different kinds of housing but for different strategies of land management and place-making. In the center city, where for fifty years our efforts at rebuilding have largely been miserable failures, we must discover ways to recapture the public street for the public, to evolve a language of form that sees the street wall not merely as a collection of private facades but also as public scenography. In the middle city, we must begin by reexamining those pre–World War II models of metropolitan urbanism, the so-called streetcar suburbs, which were tied to the city grid and public transportation system yet had distinct physical characteristics that reinforced neighborhood identities, creating something remarkably livable and occasionally artistic. I am thinking of Brookline outside Boston, Chestnut Hill in Philadelphia, or Sunnyside in Queens, New York.

In the outer suburbs, the failings of the conventional subdivision are well-documented, yet we continue to rape the land and create noplace non–places. But how far can our cities reach out? How much can they grab before their plans cease to resemble integrated organisms and become doughnuts of prosperity with empty centers?

In an age in which the whirlpool-bath-for-two and the three-car garage have come to substitute for satisfying domestic accommodation, it is hard to be optimistic about the design of housing. Progress in material comforts there may be, but if architecture sets the stage for the drama of daily life, that drama has vastly outstripped the setting. Though the projects in this book suggest that good architecture does have the capacity to elevate mere shelter into something special, what is on these pages represents but an infinitesimal portion of what is being built – and the large mass of housing being built in America today is pretty appalling. But even the best work does not go far enough. What is needed everywhere where people gather together, whether to live, work, or whatever, is more than improved designs for individual projects. What is needed is a renewed understanding that housing is an environmental and cultural act.

As architects, we have the obligation to know the best of what has been done before and we must set out to at least rival the achievements of the past. Most of all, we have a responsibility to make art out of the circumstances of ordinary living.

Robert A.M. Stern, FAIA

AMERICAN INSTITUTE OF ARCHITECTS
1990 HOUSING PUBLICATION JURY

Larry Cole, president
Larry Cole Companies, Bedford, TX

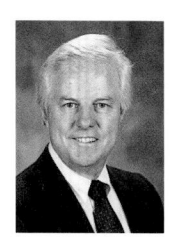

Bruce Downing, AIA, founding principal
Downing Thorpe & James, Boulder, CO

John V. Mutlow, AIA, principal
John V. Mutlow Architects, Los Angeles, CA
Professor, University of Southern California

Mitchell Rouda, editor
Builder, National Association
of Home Builders, Washington, DC

Paul Sachner, executive editor
Architectural Record, New York, NY

Daniel Solomon, FAIA, founding principal
Represented by Kathryn Clarke, principal
Solomon, Inc., San Francisco, CA

Robert A.M. Stern, FAIA
founder and senior partner
Represented by Paul L. Whalen, partner
Robert A.M. Stern Architects New York, NY

James W. Wentling, AIA, principal
James Wentling Architects, Philadelphia, PA
Chairman, AIA Housing Committee, 1990

Preface

Housing is and probably always will be the mainstay of architecture. In 19th-century cities housing provided the physical and visual continuity that held the urban fabric together. Scale and population density reinforced the connectedness of the pedestrian environment. In this century, the single-family suburban house has come to be equated with the values of home and family. In fulfilling a quest for privacy and individual self-expression, it has also become an icon. Simultaneously urban sprawl has made the road or street the binding element of the city and the automobile has displaced the pedestrian.

Today changing values and new lifestyles are demanding alternative forms of housing that offer a variety of dwelling types within friendly, pedestrian-oriented environments. The custom-designed single-family house, with its exploration of new ideas and forms, receives wide recognition in both the architectural and the popular press. Yet single-family production housing, multi-family housing, and housing designed within community and master plans are the primary forms of shelter.

This book and the competition on which it is based were initiated by the Committee on Housing of the American Institute of Architects (AIA) to increase awareness of exemplary housing design in all these categories. At a meeting in September 1990 the jury reviewed 115 submissions and selected 24 projects for publication. (These are headed by "Excellence," "Merit," or "Mention.") The jury also chose several additional projects with noteworthy elements for inclusion in the book. The selection was then expanded beyond the competition by adding projects that express alternative viewpoints or ideas or fill typological gaps. The projects are assigned to four categories – the custom single-family home, single-family multiple and production housing (including "semi-custom"), multi-family housing, and community and master plan housing. Of these the first three show only built work.

This book is intended as the first of a series, to be based on a biennial AIA review. We think that the projects presented here demonstrate recent possibilities for innovation and quality in housing design. We hope that this volume and the ones that follow will bring attention to and increase demand for a variety of dwelling types and places.

John V. Mutlow, AIA

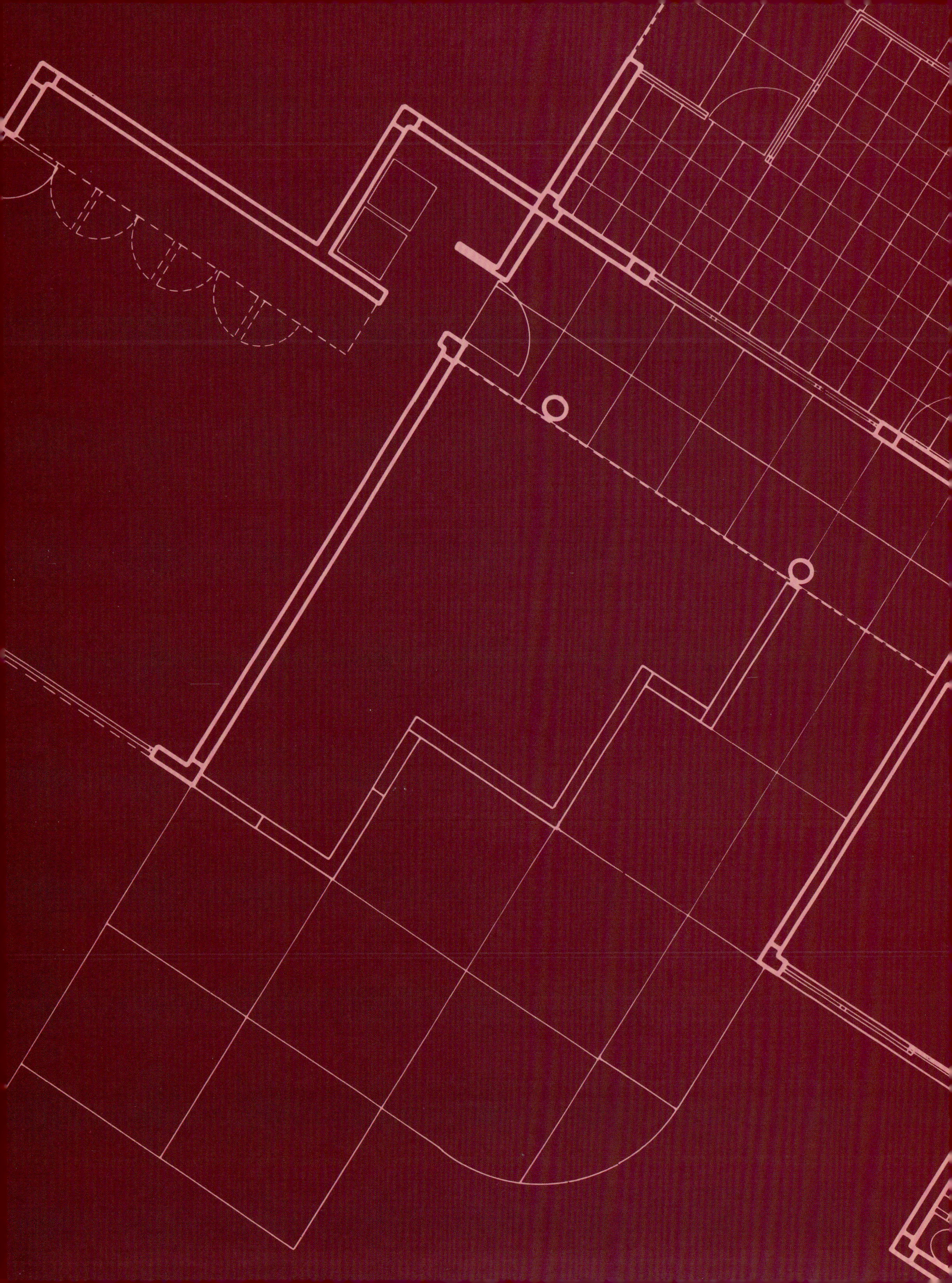

The Custom Single-Family Home

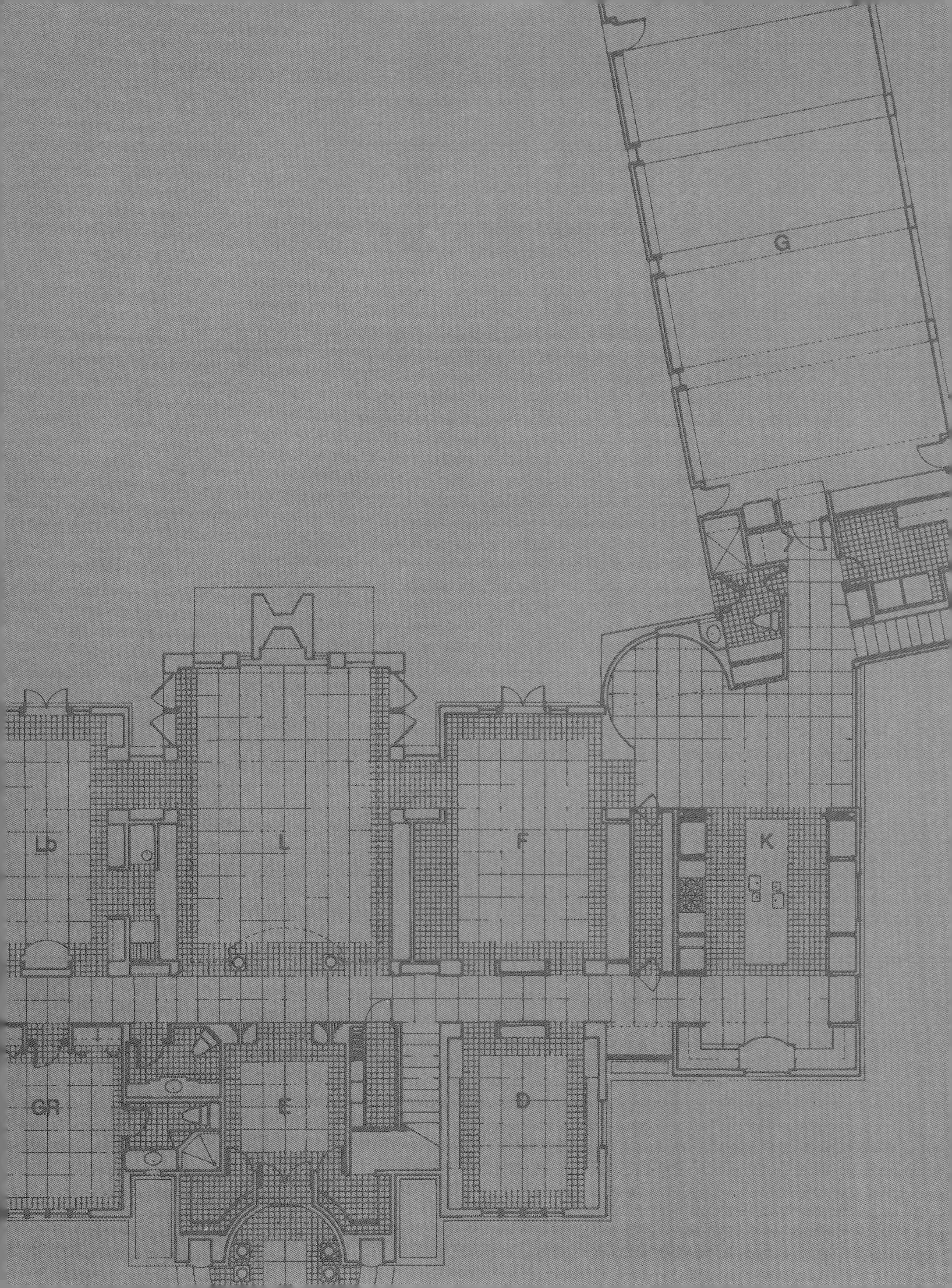
G
Lb
L
F
K
GR
E
D

The Custom Single-Family Home

The custom single-family house is still the American dream. Even though to idealists it is obvious that society would benefit from the extra open space if everyone lived in apartments or town houses, most Americans, now as before, prefer to live in a detached house. Most also would prefer a house that is custom designed for their needs, but probably less than 5 percent of all new houses in the United States are custom designed. Conversely, the media attention directed to custom houses greatly exceeds that given to any other kind of housing.

Custom house design has always offered the opportunity for experimentation in new lifestyles, but the realization has been far less than the potential. The design of a custom house requires maintaining a delicate balance among the client's needs, desires, and budget. Add to this striking an equally important balance between the client's and the architect's ideas and egos, and the result is a potential for chaos as well as for a beautifully original design.

For the architect of custom houses the challenge has never been greater. Even those who can afford a custom house in an urban or suburban area are forced to face the necessity of building on smaller parcels of land. As house lots have become smaller and more expensive, architects have had to become more creative, designing small spaces to borrow from each other visually while maintaining areas of privacy. Meanwhile, as the designer's palette in architectural direction, technology, and materials expands at an ever-increasing rate, architects must also discriminate among trends and continue to be leaders in establishing design standards that transcend the latest architectural fads.

Don Jacobs, AIA

Excellence

Photography: Robert C. Lautman

This house is sited on the edge of a cliff, overlooking a grove of coconut palms growing out of the delta formed by one of the many clear, freshwater rivers that flow into the Caribbean Sea.

Reflecting the scale and forms of the houses in the nearby fishing village of Bahibe, the corridor-free, 7-pavilion house looks out at the ever-changing light of the sea across a swimming pool. Its view is defined by the formal podium on which it rests, and all but one of its major rooms share it. Some spaces enjoy three and even four exposures. contd.

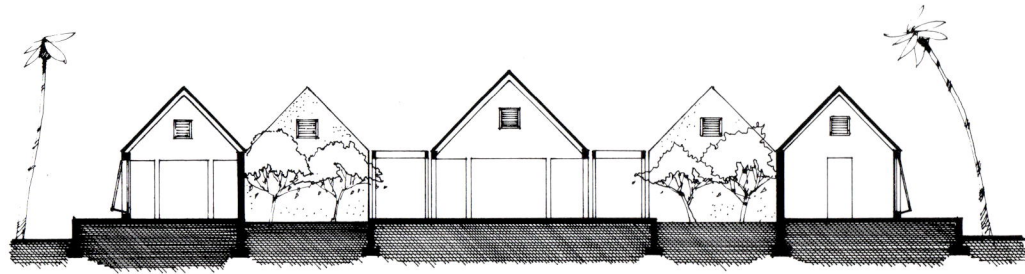

EAST/WEST SECTION

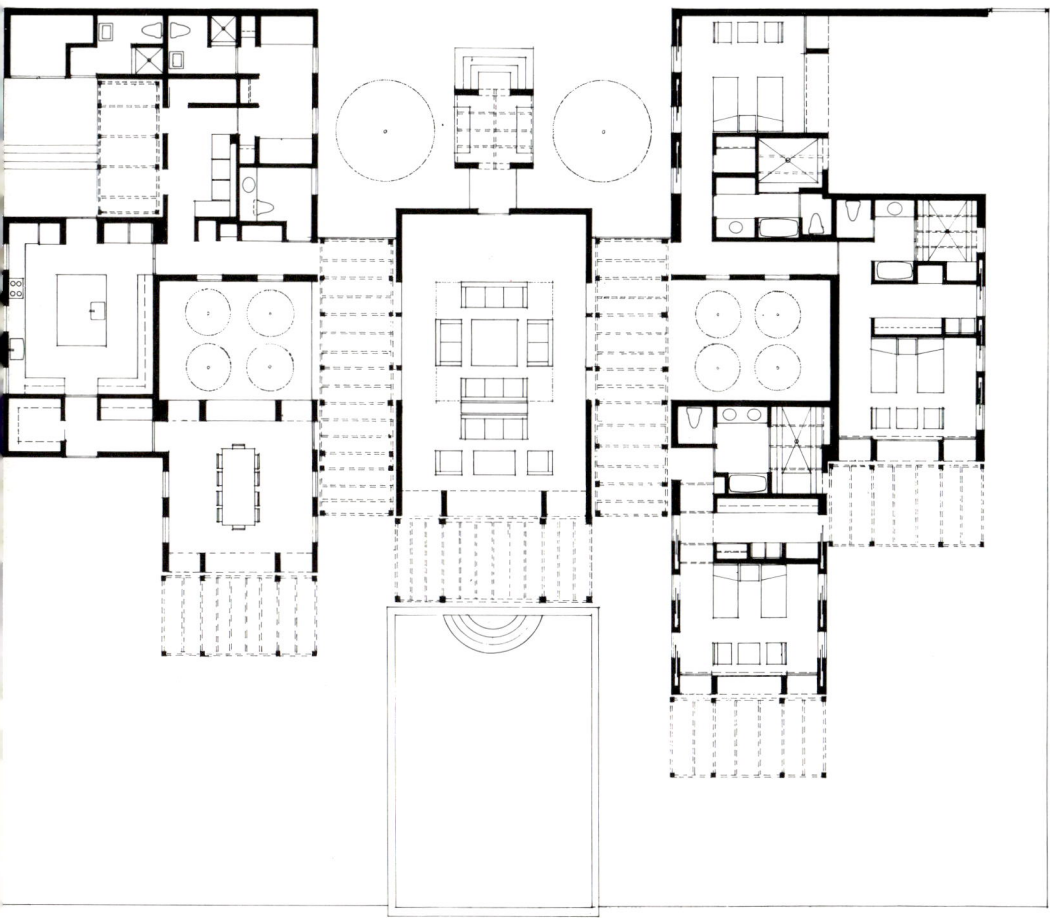

PROJECT
Residence in La Romana
Dominican Republic

ARCHITECT
Hugh Newell Jacobsen, FAIA
2529 P Street NW
Washington, DC 20007
Telephone (202) 337 5200

Project Architects
John Murphey and Ernest Schichler

OWNER
Mr. & Mrs. Eugenio Mendoza
New York, NY

Size and Capacity
Number of units - 1
Gross square feet - 6,630
Ratio of gross: Net - 5,000

Construction Type
New

Construction Cost
N/A

Status
Complete, May 1987

Engineers
McMullan & Associates
Vienna, VA
Structural Engineer

Landscape Architect
Hugh Newell Jacobsen, FAIA
Washington, DC

Contractor
Ing. Fernando Le Brun
La Romana
Dominican Republic

Photography: Robert C. Lautman

The furniture, lighting devices, and weather vane were all specifically designed and fabricated in the Dominican Republic for this island home. The floors, indeed the entire podium, are surfaced with a white, travertine-like marble quarried on the island. The seven buildings and the screen walls are made of stucco applied over the local cinder block, which is capable of resisting hurricane winds. The roofs are made of imported cedar shingles applied over expressed purlins.

An eighth pavilion serves as an entry; roofless, its exposed rafters were designed to filter the Caribbean sun.

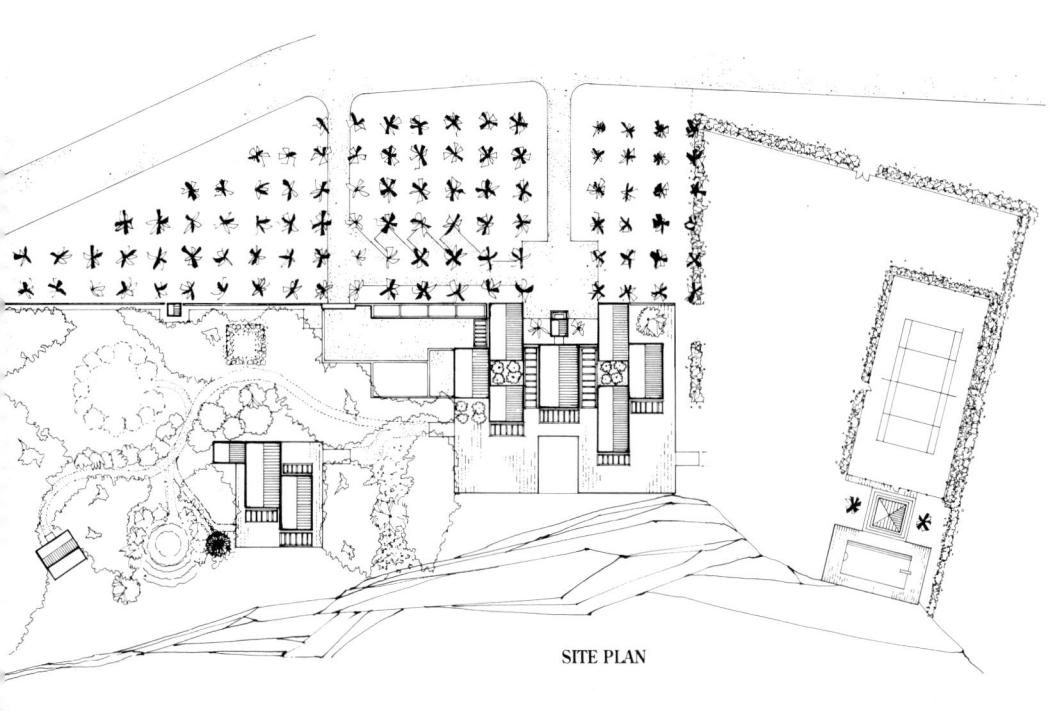

SITE PLAN

FIRST LEVEL

Merit

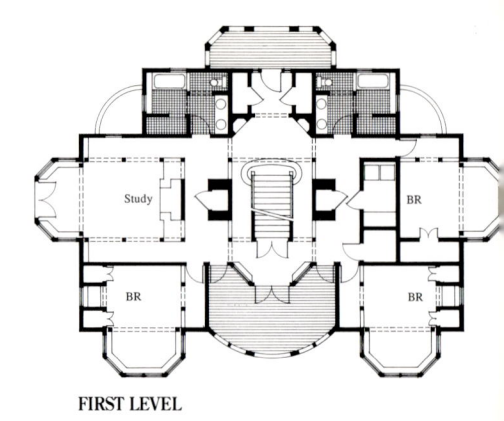

The main house is located on a corner site on the outskirts of a small, densely settled village on Nantucket. A garage/guest house was sited between the main house and the street to define the entry driveway and the private side lawn. To further screen the house from nearby streets, a thick hedge was planted along the two exposed edges of the property.

To capture views of the ocean, the two-and-a-half-story house was designed with the main living areas on the second floor. From the front door, a vestibule and central stair lead to the second-level main living room, dining room, library, study, and kitchen. The first floor has three bedrooms, two baths, a laundry room, a screened porch, and a large study, which opens to the south lawn. The private third floor has built-in bookshelves and desk at the stair landing, a master bedroom with fireplace, and a bath with two adjacent dressing areas.

The house has a natural shingle exterior and double-hung windows in keeping with strict guidelines established by the island's Historic District Commission. The roof is composed of interlocking gables, maximizing ocean views from the second level. Decorative shingle banding enlivens the facade and corbeled chimneys and chimney pots provide a vertical accent to the house's gabled silhouette.

On the interior, wood trim accents the spatial organization of the house by topping beams and columns with a lighted spindle balustrade. Stile-and-rail interior doors have etched-glass panes, bringing light into corridor and hall areas. Wood casework throughout the house establishes a wainscot and becomes, in various areas, window seats, room dividers, desks, and cabinets.

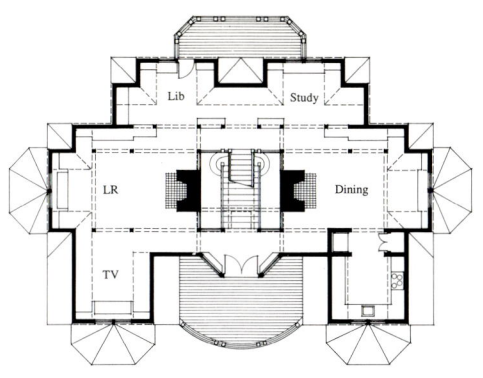

SECOND LEVEL

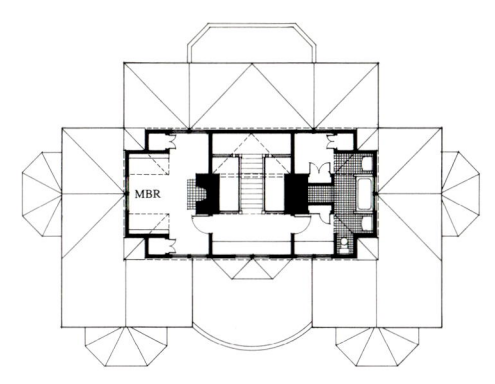

THIRD LEVEL

TRANSVERSE SECTION

Photography: Nick Wheeler

PROJECT
Nantucket house
Nantucket, MA

ARCHITECT
Architectural Resources
Cambridge, Inc.
140 Mount Auburn Street
Cambridge, MA
Telephone (617) 547 2200

OWNER
N/A

Size and Capacity
Number of units - 1
Ratio of gross: Net - 1:1

Construction Type
New

Construction Cost
N/A

Status
Complete, September 1988

Engineer
John Born Associates
Cambridge, MA
Structural Engineer

Contractor
Hill Construction
Nantucket, MA

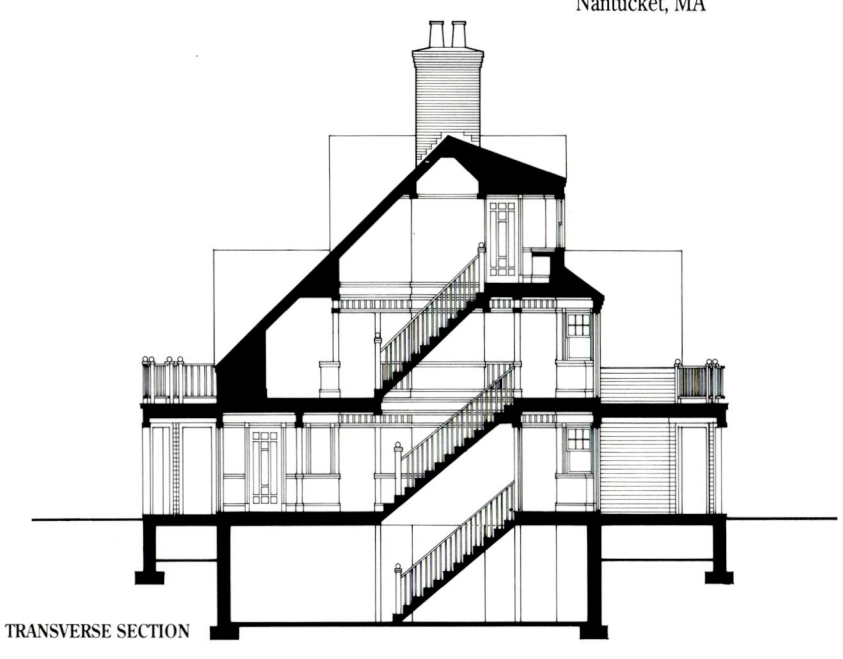

19

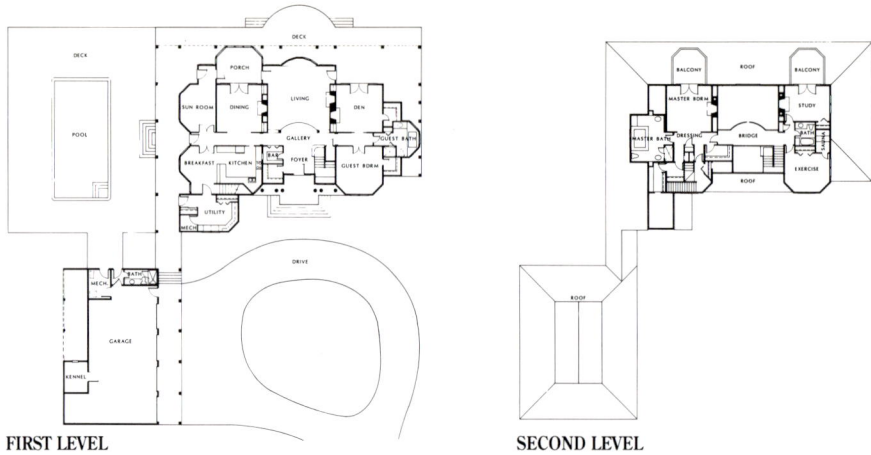

FIRST LEVEL

SECOND LEVEL

SITE PLAN

Merit

This twenty-acre site is located on the Eastern Shore of Maryland at the juncture of the Wicomico River and Wicomico Creek, twelve miles from the city of Salisbury. The Wicomico Yacht Club is located on the adjacent property to the south. Other neighboring properties consist of single-family homes or farms on waterfront sites of similar size.

This house is a symbol of repose for the busy couple who inhabit it. One owner has fond memories of her grandmother's farmhouse, especially the "secret" stair through which she was able to run from floor to floor up to the treasured attic retreat. The house recaptures that spirit with a winding service stair to an upper level retreat.

The location next to the Yacht Club, as well as the size of the site, inspired a house that could become a landmark from the river, especially at night. This idea, coupled with that of the stair and the attic retreat, generated the tower as the culmination of the stair and an identifying element for approaching vessels. The continuous veranda extends the house into the landscape and provides a transitional outdoor living space. First floor circulation extends through the gallery while the master bedroom suite is connected to the rest of the house by the second floor bridge.

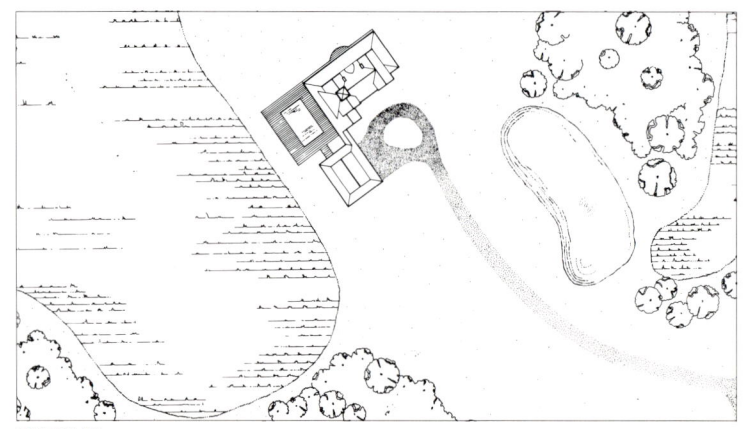

PROJECT
Kleger residence
Wicomico County, MD

ARCHITECT
Becker/Morgan Architects Inc.
312 West Main Street
Salisbury, MD 21803
Telephone (301) 546 9100

Principal in Charge
W. Ronald Morgan, AIA

Design Architect
Susan C. Wigley, AIA

OWNER
Dr. and Mrs. Sheldon Kleger
Wicomico County, MD

Size and Capacity
Number of units - 1
Gross square feet - 6,420
Ratio of gross: Net - 4,820:3,730 or 77%

Construction Type
New

Status
Complete, November 1989

Engineer
Morabito Consultants Inc.
Baltimore, MD
Structural Engineer

Contractor
Bunting Construction Corporation
Selbyville, DE

Photography: Gary Marine Photography

Merit

Two long, glass-walled pavilions drawn across this coastal site at the juncture of dense forest and open meadow strengthen and articulate the natural division of the landscape. At a break between the pavilions, two massive stone chimneys form a gateway, allowing passage from the lush woods to the barren ocean front and directing entry into the house.

Divided into family accommodations and guest quarters, the spaces are intentionally very simple in their organization and geometric form. This simplicity frames and sets off the remarkable natural setting – on one side the immediate miniature landscape of rocks and mosses on the forest floor and on the other the sheer, dramatic landscape of sparse grass, black basalt ledges, and open sea.

Structurally and formally the building is a series of transverse bearing walls carrying the roof deck. The walls are pierced by large and small openings to provide a sequence of varied spaces. Free of any load-bearing function, the exterior longitudinal walls are made up entirely of sliding glass panels framed in teak and mahogany. All of the interior and exterior surfaces are of wood–cedar, mahogany, or douglas fir.

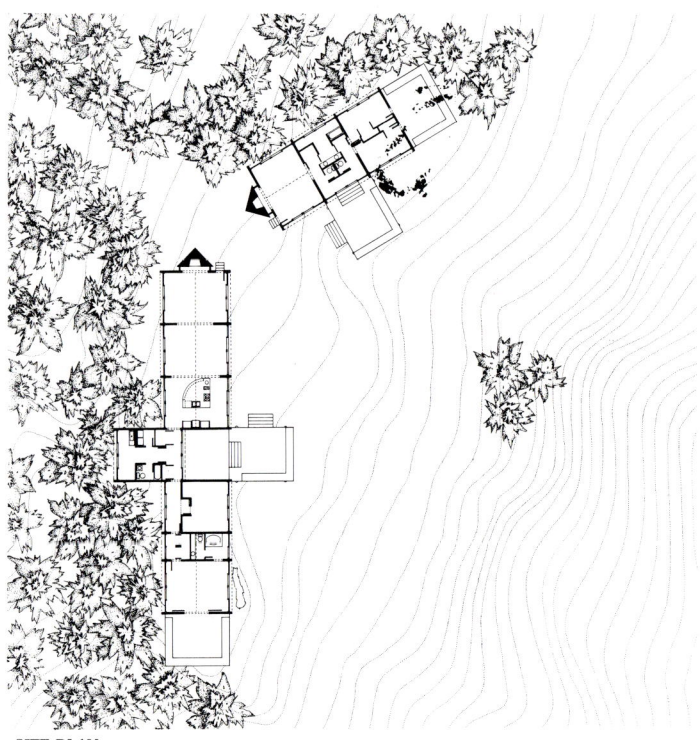

SITE PLAN

PROJECT
Ward house
Great Cranberry Island, ME

ARCHITECT
Peter Forbes and Associates, Inc.
241 A Street
Boston, MA 02210
Telephone (617) 542 1760

OWNER
Mr. and Mrs. Rodman Ward
Wilmington, DE

Size and Capacity
Number of units - 1
Gross square feet - 3,040

Construction Type
New

Construction Cost
N/A

Status
Complete, November 1987

Engineers
Zaldastani Associates, Inc.
Boston, MA
Structural Engineer

Peter Forbes and Associates, Inc.
Boston, MA
Mechanical Engineer

Contractors
Victor Mercer, Inc.
& Michael Westfall
Southwest Harbor, ME

Photography: Timothy Hursley

23

Merit

In an affluent community of stately mansions south of San Francisco, this house draws on the traditional architecture of its neighbors yet stands on its own as a modern villa. The architect balanced the design constraints and opportunities presented by a client who wanted the best of both traditional and contemporary architecture. The program objectives are achieved through careful planning and a thoughtful approach to detailing.

Layout and organization are characterized by symmetry, axiality, progression, and layering. It is a formal house with formal divisions of space, primary and secondary axes and circulations, and symmetry in the overall plan and within the rooms. Progression within the house leads through layers of composed facades with vistas to and beyond each space and focus. The major rooms spill onto sun-drenched terraces, pool, spa, and gardens enclosed by stands of mature trees.

contd.

Photography: Gerald Ratto

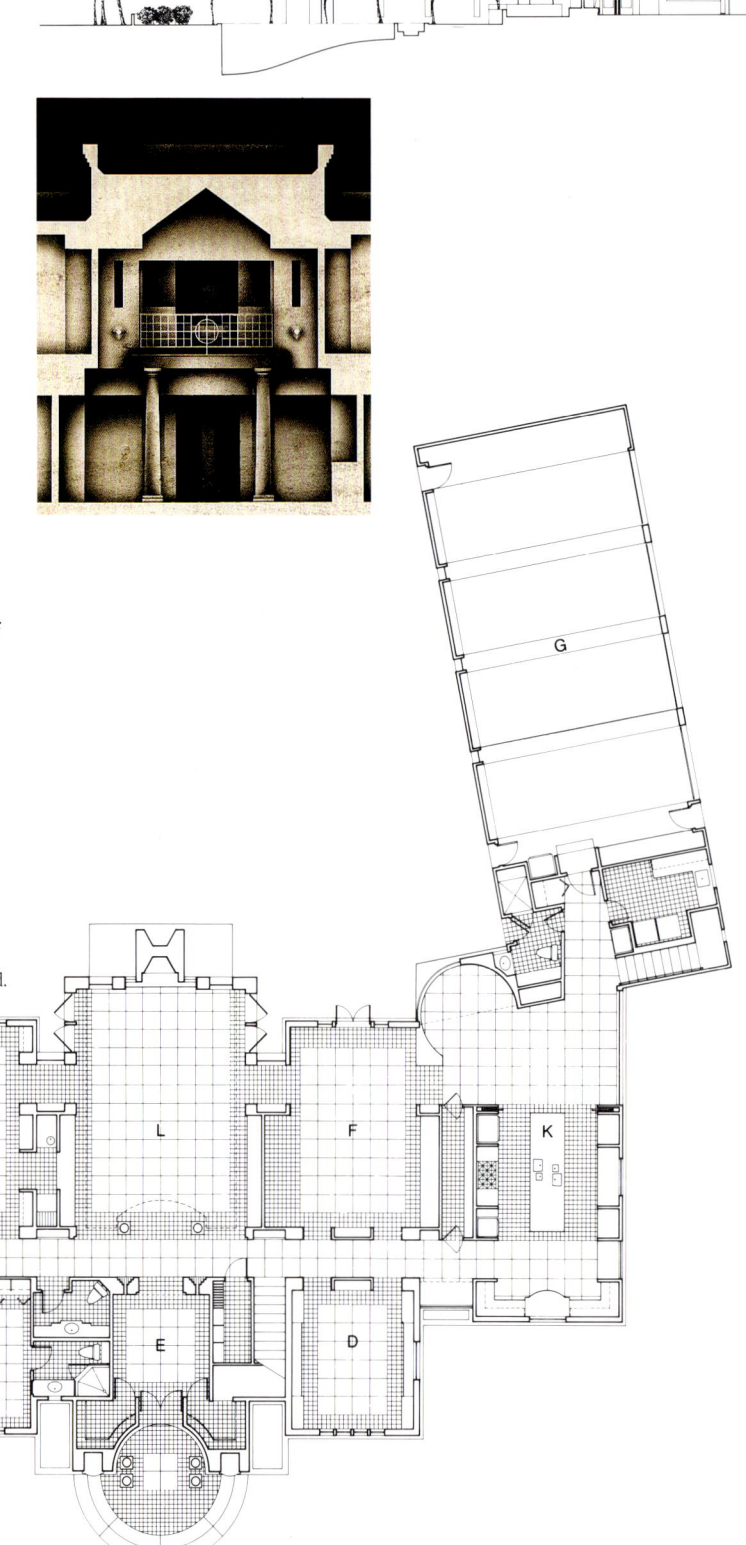

FIRST LEVEL

PROJECT
Gersch residence
Hillsborough, CA

ARCHITECT
House + House
1499 Washington Street
San Francisco, CA 94109
Telephone (415) 474 2112

OWNER
Seth & Barbara Gersch
Hillsborough, CA

Size and Capacity
Number of units - 1
Gross square feet - 9,465
Ratio of gross: Net - 95%

Construction Type
New

Status
Complete, June 1988

Engineer
Geoffrey F. Barrett
Mill Valley, CA
Structural Engineer

Consultant
Novella Smith
San Francisco, CA
Lighting Consultant

Contractor
Covert & Associates
Nevada City, CA

SITE PLAN

25

Creative construction detailing using the rough framing and sheetrock to achieve the most drama afforded the use of some finer materials. Double-framed walls give a sense of solidity and a sculptural quality. The play of light and shadows on the thick walls is further enhanced by soffiting, articulation, and varying ceiling heights. Special touches give the house its elegance, such as the limestone paving, columns, and fireplace, the copper pyramid at the entry, and the custom-designed front door and railings. The stucco is hand rubbed to the luster of limestone, and the interior walls are faux painted for the same effect.

The architectural features are classical in form yet modern in treatment. The house is an elegant showplace for large-scale entertaining as well as an exhilarating home with spacious, private, outdoor living space.

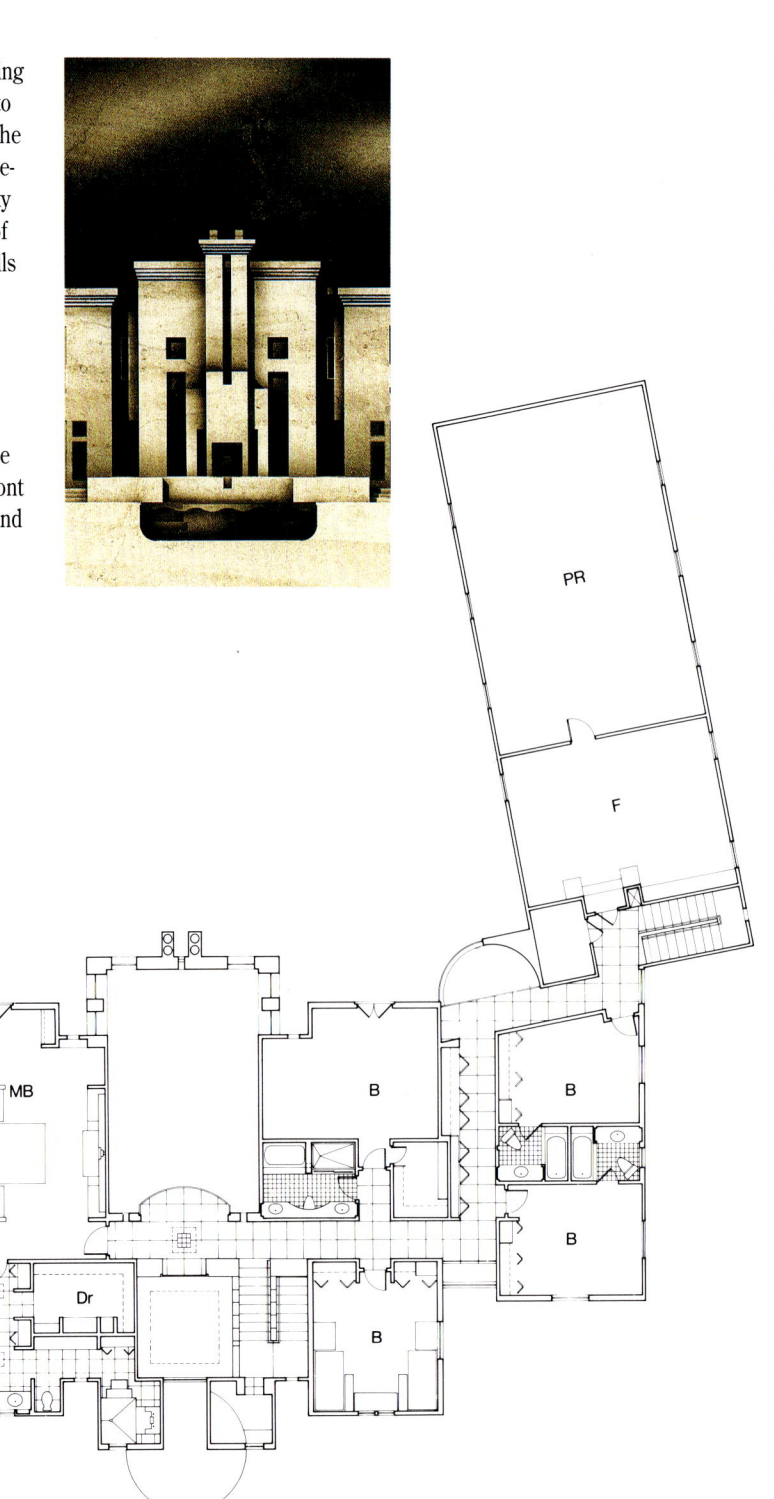

SECOND LEVEL

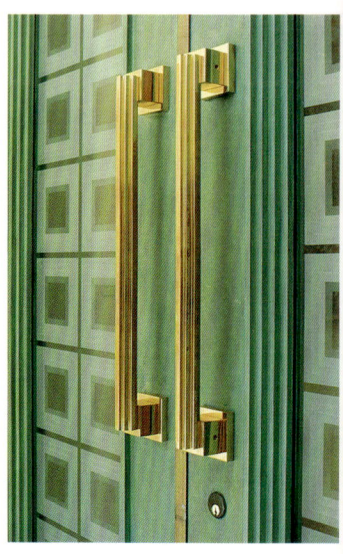

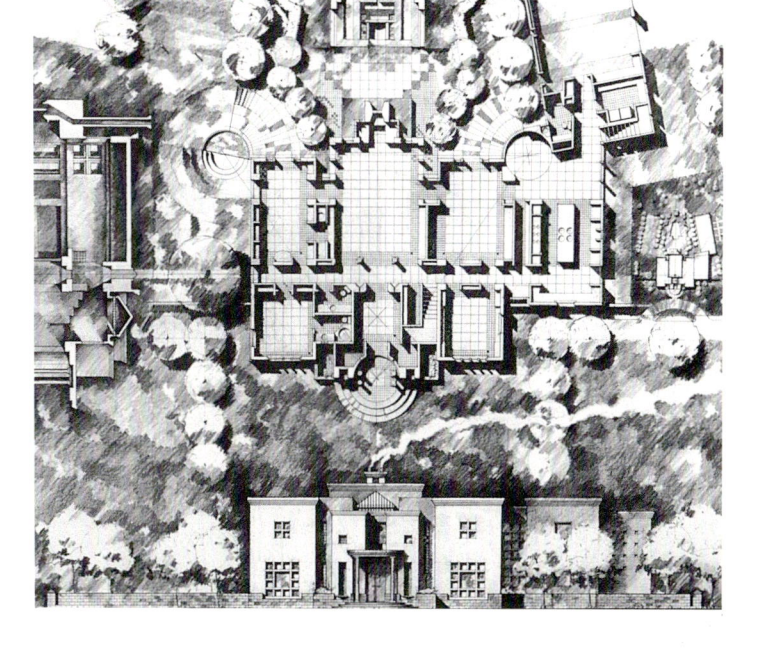

Photography: Gerald Ratto

27

■ *Merit*

This house is sited in a broad and open meadow between a large, old oak and an expanse of open cove that leads to Long Island Sound. The oak and the architecture combine to hide the water until it is framed by the house, which turns the strong, central axis formed by the entrance drive and the chimney mass 45 degrees toward the cove and the view.

The design of this house is disciplined by an implied order based on a single square, with multiples forming larger squares, double squares, and so on; and the rooflines follow the diagonals of the squares.

Designed in six parts, with its entry and stair enclosed separately, the house is composed of successive pavilions that are tightly aligned in symmetrical pairs at their gable ends. The pavilion facades match one another as they shrink in size, maintaining a balance on either side of the chimney mass. Each pavilion houses an individual function, and three of the pavilions contain second floor spaces.

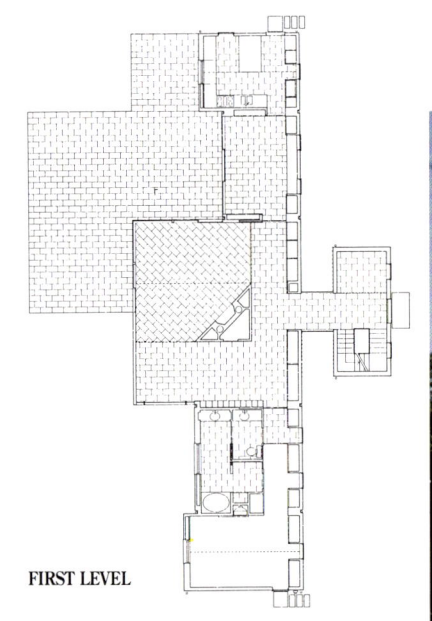

FIRST LEVEL

PROJECT
Palmedo residence
St. James, NY

ARCHITECT
Hugh Newell Jacobsen, FAIA
2529 P Street NW
Washington, DC 20007
Telephone (202) 337 5200

Project Architect
Charles P. Parker

OWNER
Mr. and Mrs. Philip Palmedo
St. James, NY

Size and Capacity
Number of units - 1
Gross square feet - 4,724
Ratio of gross: Net - 4,251

Construction Type
New

Construction Cost
N/A

Status
Completed, June 1988

Engineer
MMP International
Washington, DC
Structural Engineer

Consultant
Hugh Newell Jacobsen, FAIA
Washington, DC
Landscape Architect

Contractor
Van Horn & Son Ltd.
Setauket, NY

Photography: Robert C. Lautman

Merit

The clients for this residence purchased the site, located within the city limits, for its exciting garden ruins left from an early 20th century estate. Although they liked the formal gardens, the owners did not want a grand house or an estate. They wanted a house that had the image of a cottage from the exterior and felt bright, open and airy on the interior.

The owners emphasized to the architects that they wanted a comfortable house, open to spectacular views of the gardens and woods beyond. The design idea for the house grew in response to the formal and symmetrical configuration of the existing garden and the owners' request that the house accommodate their informal lifestyle.

The house is designed in a linear configuration parallel to the gardens, with a circulation spine extending the length of the house. This corridor acts as a buffer to an adjacent apartment complex visible in winter on the hillside above. The front facade of the house is a formal elevation, designed as a straight wall with minimal openings and softened by an entrance porch. It also becomes one wall of a parking court, which is formed by an existing retaining wall and the future garage.

A cross axis is formed by a 2-story space centered on the main garden entrance and linking the front door of the house to doors on the rear elevation. The elevation of the house that faces the gardens is a less formal composition, open with glazing and views to the garden and southwest sunlight.

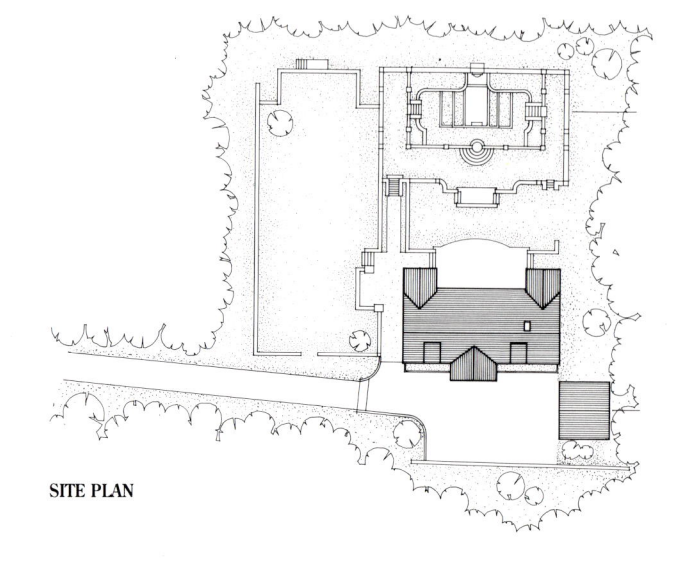

SITE PLAN

PROJECT
Chestnut Hill residence
Philadelphia, PA

ARCHITECT
Susan Maxman Architects
123 S. 22nd Street
Philadelphia, PA
Telephone (215) 977 8662

OWNER
N/A

Size and Capacity
Number of units - 1
Gross square feet - 5,500

Construction Type
New

Status
Complete, June 1989

Engineers
Ortega Consulting
Media, PA
Structural Engineer

Bruce E. Brooks & Associates
Philadelphia, PA
Mechanical and Electrical Engineer

Contractor
Cornerstone Construction
Rosemont, PA

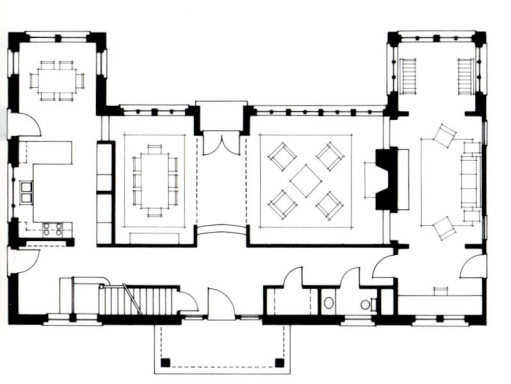

Photography: Tom Bernard

FIRST LEVEL

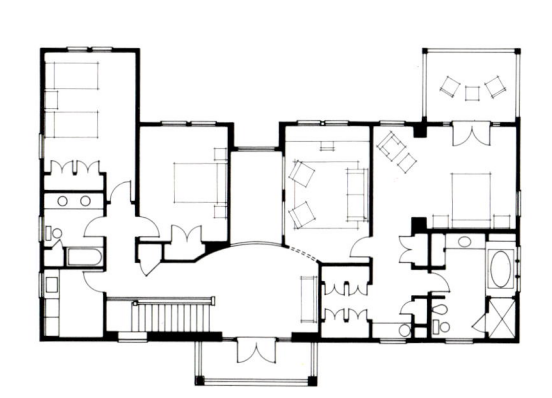

SECOND LEVEL

31

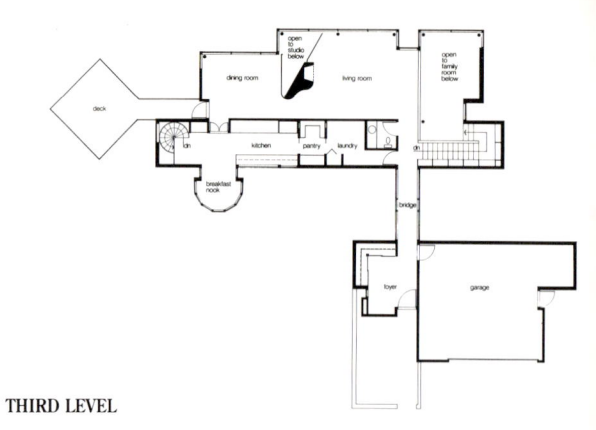

Merit

THIRD LEVEL

An architect, his artist wife, and three children wanted to build a new four-bedroom home on a steep heavily wooded lot, which focuses on a small spring-fed pond to the north. The two older children were infrequent visitors from college and the youngest child had approximately five more years living at home. The characteristics of the site determined that the house would be broken into two components connected by a bridge. The foyer and garage component connects to the main house, which contains steps down the hill and a public level on top, a private level with family space in the middle, and a lower level for the children (which can be closed off when they are away).

A desire to live in nature, with privacy, generated a plan in which all service spaces are organized into a tight core. This core buffers the living spaces from the road and is built into the hill, making it possible for each living space to interact with nature via a glass wall on the north.

This northern orientation brings wonderful, soft light into the artist studio as well as the other major living spaces. The placement of the house and outdoor decks was carefully planned to retain virtually every tree on site in an attempt to engage nature and extend its beauty into the interior spaces.

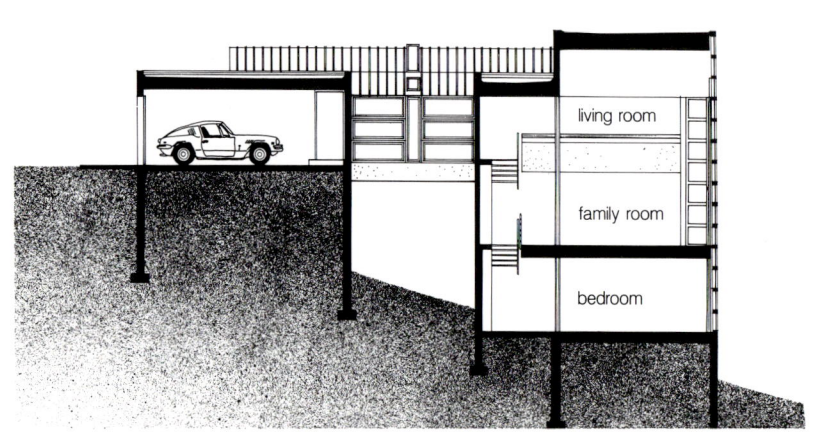

SITE PLAN

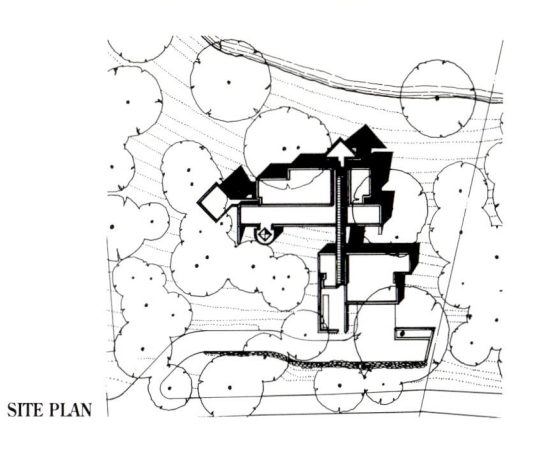

Photography: Timothy Hursley

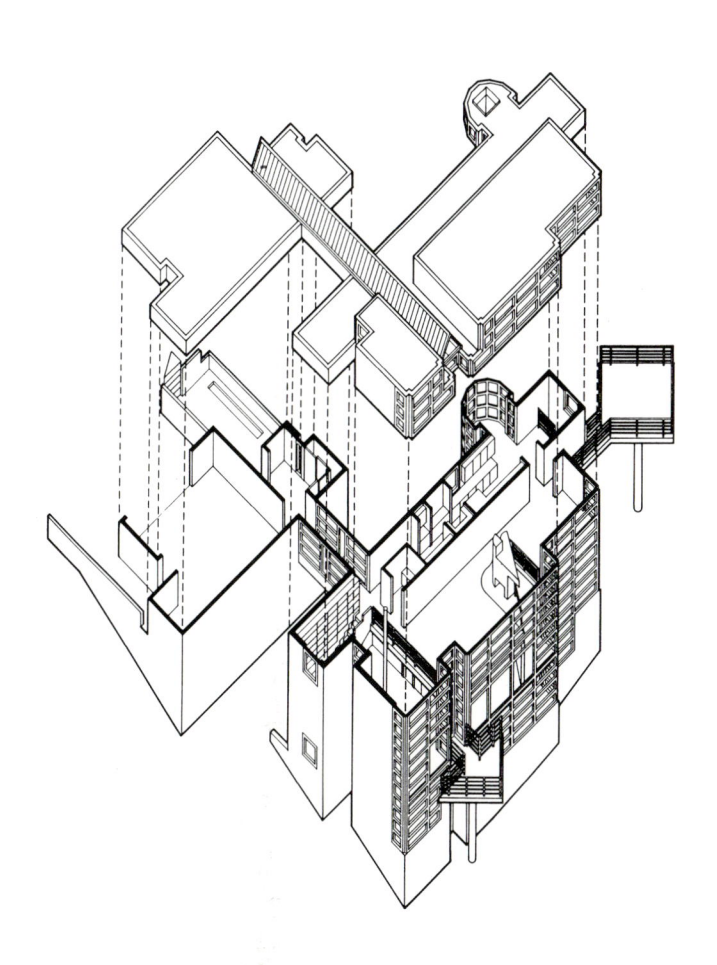

PROJECT
Neumann residence
Franklin, MI

ARCHITECT
Kenneth Neumann/Joel Smith
and Associates, Inc.
400 Galleria Officentre
Suite 555
Southfield, MI 48034
Telephone (313) 352 8310

OWNER
Kenneth and Beverly Neumann
Franklin, MI

Size and Capacity
Number of units - 1
Gross square feet - 5,000

Construction Type
New

Construction Cost
$450,000

Status
Complete, October 1988

Engineers
Ehlert/Bryan, Inc.
Southfield, MI
Structural Engineer

MCS Associates, Inc.
Sterling Heights, MI
Civil Engineer

Consultant
John Grissim & Associates, Inc.
Farmington Hills, MI
Landscape Architect

Contractor
Wineman & Komer
Building Company
Southfield, MI

33

Mention

This apartment-sized residence (1,500 square feet) is located in town on a small lot (50'x100') edged with neighboring residences and street traffic.

The design responds to its urban location and the Florida sunlight (which is both friend and foe) as well as program requirements for spaces that are open, bright, cool, and private. Additional requirements were for spaces that could be economically air-conditioned, and a form that clearly belonged to the semitropical Central Florida region.

Bright sunlight, warm days, and warm nights are the prevailing issues of the Central Florida climate. The construction is heavily insulated light wood framing that will resist daytime heat transmission and not store it for transmission into the building during the warm evenings and nights. The near white exterior reflects sunlight while deep overhangs shade the openings.

A louver system located at the bottom of the roof overhangs mediates the transition to the glazed openings below. The louvers increase the shading of the openings while providing a view filter that masks undesirable scenes and increases the interior sense of privacy. The wide, flat design of the louvers also allows them to serve as a light shelf, which diffuses and reflects a portion of the light to the interior.

Small, walled courtyards at each end of the living-dining space allow it to be opened for air movement and to extend the space visually without loss of privacy. The close proximity of the courtyard walls, their light coloration, and the white tile horizontal surfaces make "reflector wells" that contribute to the diffusion and reflection functions of the light shelf louver system above. In combination, the courtyard walls and louvers admit a measured portion of diffused light to the interior that has all the desirable characteristics of northern light.

The light value and cool gray interiors make the most of the admitted light by reflecting and distributing it farther into the interior spaces.

Ten foot high ceilings allow stratification of the warmest air above the occupant level. A louvered ceiling panel exhausts the warm air to the exterior or returns it to the air-conditioning system.

Miscellaneous hard and reflective materials, and finishes such as tile, marble, chrome, and dense firm carpet without padding were selected to reinforce the psychological aspects of remaining cool.

Photography: George Cott

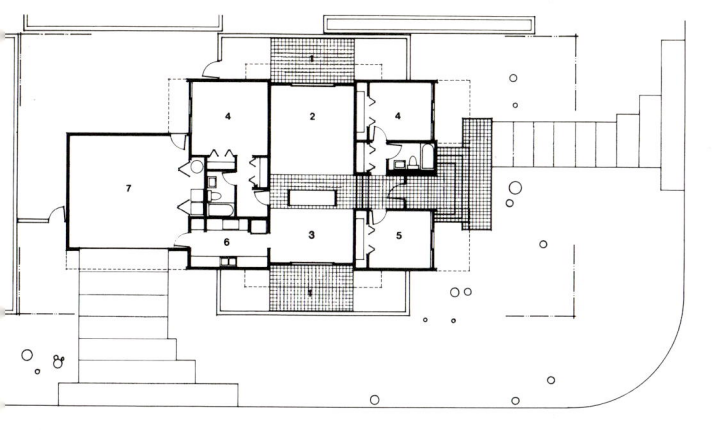

1. Courtyard
2. Living
3. Dining
4. Bedroom
5. Study Bedroom
6. Kitchen
7. Garage

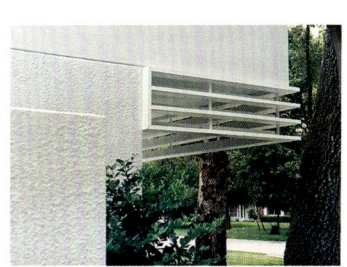

PROJECT
Rados residence
Tampa, FL

ARCHITECT
Rick Rados Architect
4223 Cleveland Street
Tampa, FL 33609
Telephone (813) 287 1548

OWNER
Rick and Sharon Rados
Tampa, FL

Size and Capacity
Number of units - 1
Gross square feet - 1,500

Construction Type
New

Construction Cost
N/A

Status
Complete, 1986

Engineers
Cabana and Fernandez
Tampa, FL
Structural Engineer

Burton and Rolley, Inc.
Tampa, FL
Mechanical and Electrical Engineer

Contractor
Ranon and Jimenez, Inc.
Tampa, FL

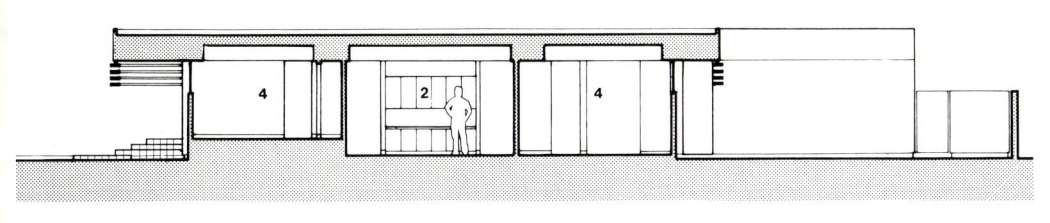

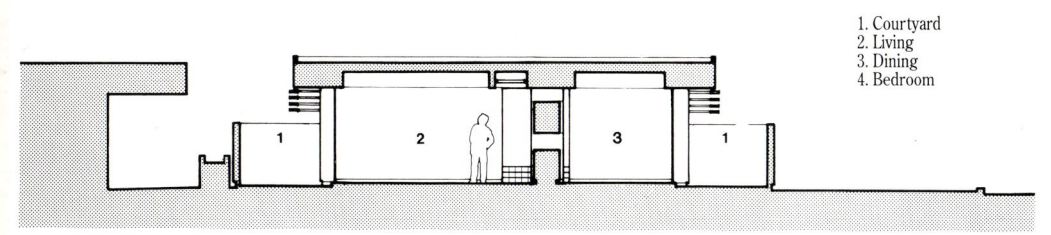

NORTH/SOUTH SECTION

1. Courtyard
2. Living
3. Dining
4. Bedroom

EAST/WEST SECTION

The decisive geometric forms with which California-based architect Frank Dimster designed adjacent residences in the Bahamas for two European families belie their flexibility and informality. The forms may be crisp and definite – a composition of International Style solids and voids – but the architect, in response to the benign climate, has relaxed the purity of the architectural cube. The profiles of these houses are broken, their volumes eroded; the houses embrace their surroundings. These are sophisticated structures that are also responsive environments; they succeed in being both urbane and casual. The wisdom of their design lies in their architectural response to climate and in their organization, the way the plan makes transitions between outside and inside and between different living areas.

Bringing the outside into a house is not a new architectural feat. There are many established ways of accomplishing this. In these houses Dimster chose to capture views, breezes, and abundant natural light and to create voluminous interiors. He established, for example, a continuous interior and exterior ground plane, separated only by glass and marked by a change in floor materials. It is, however, a fresh gesture to do the reverse: to bring the interior outside. Dimster elaborates the exterior edge of his residences to create transitional spaces that can be occupied.

In maneuvering the overall shapes of the houses to create these indoor/outdoor spaces, Frank Dimster created residences with a high ratio of exterior surface to interior volume – a ratio desirable in a hot climate.

Just as the architect used service rooms to separate areas, he used the living room as a link between the bedroom wings. In both residences, bedroom suites are situated on opposite sides of the living room. These suites, each with outside entrance, function as small, semiautonomous apartments within the larger house, giving guests and family the choice of being independent. Dimster purposely designed these bedroom wings as ambivalent spaces integral to, yet separate from, the main body of the house. He did not overcommit them as sleeping areas, but kept them ambiguous enough so they can be used as studies.

While Dimster designed two houses that respond to the warm Bahamian climate with an outside edge of habitable spaces, he also defended the houses against the sometimes inclement seasons. The white stucco surface makes the buildings look abstract, but the stucco resists the penetration of water into the wall materials, and the white resists the insistent tropical sun.

While Dimster oriented the houses to the water for the view, he also protected the facades from the occasional hurricanes that come off the ocean. He accomplished this by building a detached structure with vertical fins in front of the sea-facing facades of each house. These structures also serve as sun screens, privacy screens, and brief buffer zones between outside and inside. Typically, Dimster put a single element, like the storm screen and skylights, to multiple use.

Like the roof forms, the screen forms visually complement the basic living volumes with another order of shapes. Although the cool, white forms could seem like objects withdrawn from their sites and aloof from their occupants, their organization sets up living patterns that take full advantage of the environmental reasons their owners have for spending time in the Bahamas.

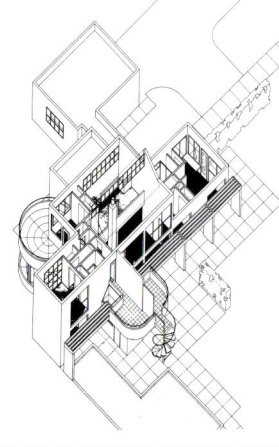

Photography: Dan Forer Photography

STAPLER RESIDENCE AXONOMETRIC

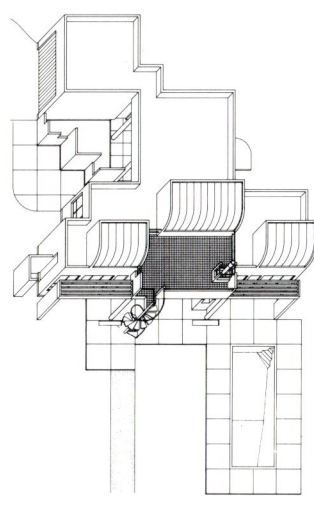

EUROCARIBBEAN RESIDENCE AXONOMETRIC

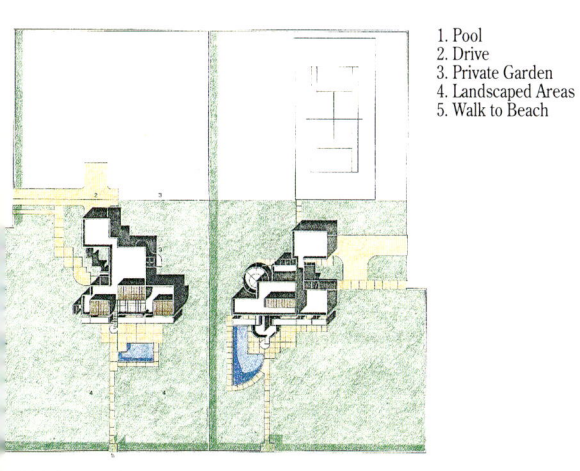

1. Pool
2. Drive
3. Private Garden
4. Landscaped Areas
5. Walk to Beach

UROCARIBBEAN AND STAPLER RESIDENCES

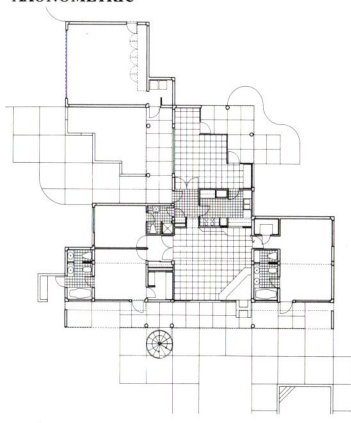

EUROCARIBBEAN RESIDENCE FIRST LEVEL

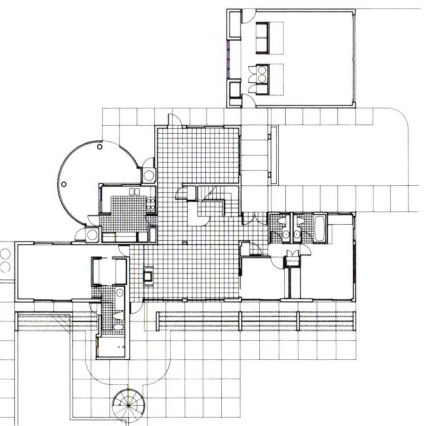

TAPLER RESIDENCE FIRST LEVEL

PROJECT
Eurocaribbean and Stapler residences
Freeport, Bahamas

ARCHITECT
Frank Dimster, AIA
1406 3/4 Kenter Avenue
Los Angeles, CA 90049
Telephone (213) 472 2079

Resident Architect
J. Moss
Freeport, Bahamas

OWNER
N/A

Size and Capacity
Number of units - 2
Gross square feet (Eurocaribbean) - 2,000
Gross square feet (Stapler) - 3,000

Construction Type
New

Construction Cost
Eurocaribbean - $250,000
Stapler - $400,000

Status
Complete, 1985

Engineers
Dimitry K. Vergun
Los Angeles, CA
Structural Engineer

Rouhy Dehbibi & Associates
Los Angeles, CA
Mechanical Engineer

Vorgias
Los Angeles, CA
Electrical Engineer

Contractor
Warren Reif Constructions
Freeport, Bahamas

Project description by
Joseph Giovannini

37

This house, located on a sloping beach site in Malibu, California, uses concrete and stone as timeless materials, to be weathered by the wind and sea like the surrounding cliffs and rocks. The house is also designed to withstand the sea; the foundation consists of concrete caissons drilled 40 feet into bedrock, providing the base for 16 concrete columns that, along with concrete beams, define the exposed frame. Stone and glass provide the infill.

The interiors are skylit. The house uses minimum energy; the concrete floors provide a solar heat sink, and cross ventilation cools the rooms.

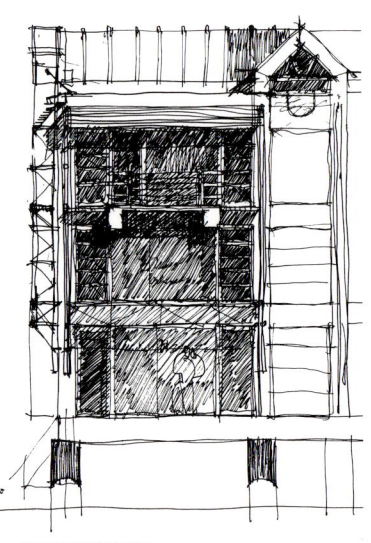

FACADE STUDY

Photography: Tim Street-Porter and Dean Pappas

WEST ELEVATION

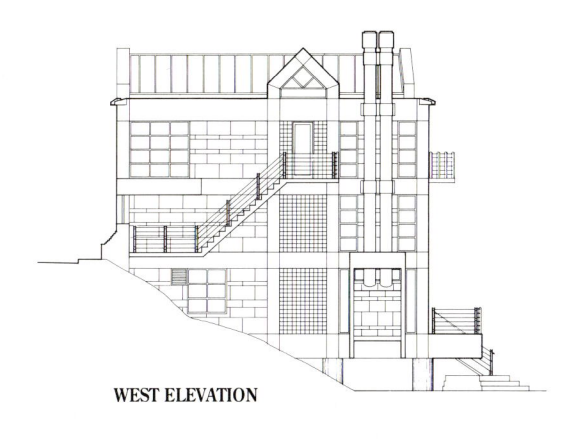

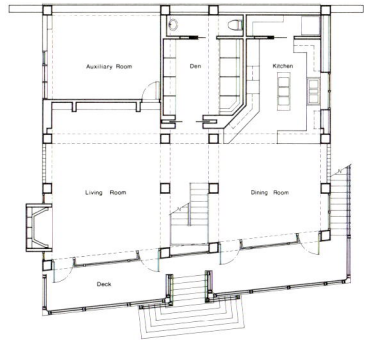

SECOND LEVEL

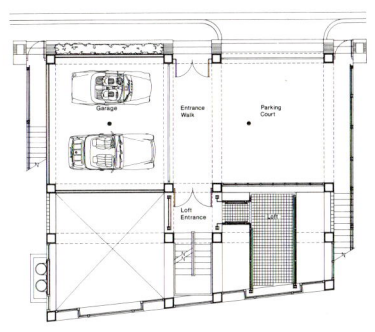

GROUND LEVEL

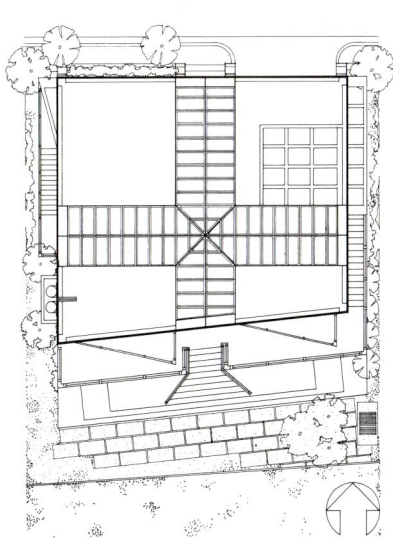

SITE PLAN

PROJECT
Gray residence
Malibu, CA

ARCHITECT
David Lawrence Gray and Associates,
Architects, AIA
1546 7th Street
Suite 300
Santa Monica, CA 90401
Telephone (310) 394 5707

OWNER
David L. & Karen L. Gray
Malibu, CA

Size and Capacity
Number of units - 1
Gross square feet - 3,157
(net of garage and carport)

Construction Type
New

Construction Cost
$950,000

Status
Complete, April 1989

Engineer
Dimitri Vergun
Santa Monica, CA
Structural Engineer

Consultant
Emmet L. Wemple & Associates
Los Angeles, CA
Landscape Architect

Contractor
LCG Construction
Malibu, CA

39

This addition to an existing Berkeley residence doubles its size and explains the relationship between site and context, old and new, public and private. The existing concrete and heavy timber structure perches on the top of a panoramic hill that is aligned with the Bay Area's spiritual Mount Tamalpais. The maverick builder of this primitive yet powerful construction created a main room with a dramatic angle of view by sloping the roof towards the view and cantilevering the floor beyond the picture windows to achieve a significant vista of the ocean and overlooking the three bridges of the Bay.

The addition makes the house a family environment. Two wings on either side of the existing structure create an interior court with a private lawn for family play. Towards the view, terraces and patios emphasize the axis of the existing concrete wall on which heavy timber beams are suspended.

The functions of the house are grouped by use and are expressed as different masses. The garage with guest quarters above serves as a barrier between the public and the private realm. The centrally located kitchen and family room on the south side are under one roof, separated from the garage/guest building by the entry, which is the extension of the traffic pattern through the house. The private sleeping areas and the bathroom on the northern part of the interior courtyard open to extensive views of the bay. The bath is built against the existing concrete retaining wall in a conscious attempt to recapture the primitive elements of the site.

The construction emphasizes the new and the old, contrasting the existing concrete and heavy timbers with the new wood construction, exaggerated in its yellowness. For the new concrete walls, similar board form walls are used to continue the tradition of the house as a primeval place of shelter and to extend the emotional pleasure of tactile and visual stimulation.

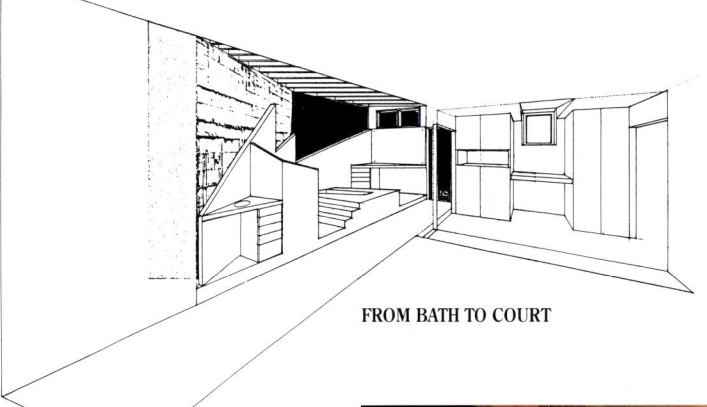

FROM BATH TO COURT

Photography: Richard Barnes

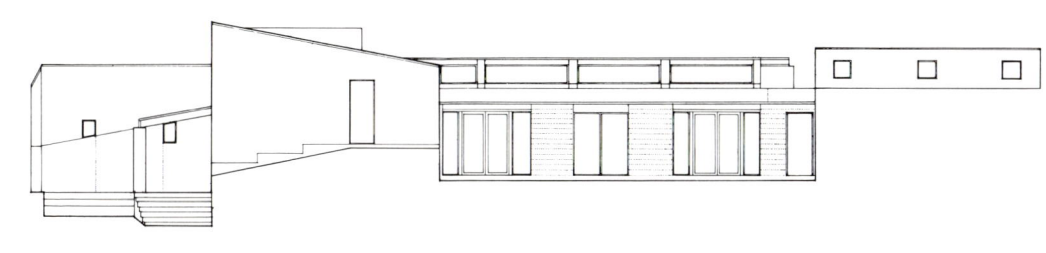

EAST ELEVATION

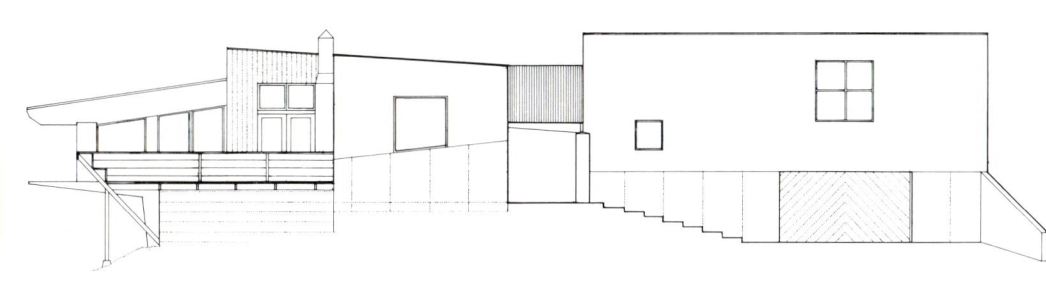

SOUTH ELEVATION

PROJECT
Baum residence
Berkeley, CA

ARCHITECT
Mark Mack
246 First Street, Suite 400
San Francisco, CA 94105
Telephone (415) 777 5305

OWNER
Jim and Laura Baum
Berkeley, CA

Size and Capacity
Number of units - 1
Gross square feet - 5,400

Construction Type
New and renovated

Construction Cost
$700,000

Status
Completed, 1987

Consultants
Vickerman Zachary/Miller
Oakland, CA
Ken Hughes
Lafayette, CA
Structural Engineer
Warm Floors
Napa, CA
Mechanical Engineer
Subsurface Consultants
Soils
Energetic Systems
Point Richmond, CA
Energy
Topher Delaney Landscape
Sausalito, CA
Landscape

Contractors
Van/Catlin Construction Company
Emeryville, CA

Located on a four-acre waterfront parcel in Edgewater (near Annapolis), Maryland, this project is a 3,000 square foot weekend residence for two *Washington Post* reporters/authors. The program requirements centered on a small house (living/dining/kitchen room, one bedroom with bath) for use by the owners each weekend, and auxiliary spaces (office, two guest bedrooms with one bath) for occasional use by the owners and their infrequent guests.

The architects' major intention was to design a residence combining formal aspects of house types found in the Annapolis region with the functional flexibility implied in the owners' program.

The residence employs the footprint of a historic plan often found in the Eastern Shore region: the five-part Maryland plan. Located in the main body of the house are the spaces to be used each weekend by the owners, while the northern and southern wings house the office and guest bedrooms/bath, respectively. The three parts of the residence are heated and cooled individually, allowing for expansion or contraction of the living spaces.

The site organization of these parts allows two different approaches. The west facade is fronted by a long tree-lined gravel drive (the final 45 seconds of a 45-minute drive from the owners' permanent residence in Georgetown) and a gravel forecourt. The east facade is fronted by a deck, lawn, and wildflowers. The main body of the residence is projected into the lawn, allowing panoramic views of the South River and Chesapeake Bay.

The exterior is composed of a red-brick base, bleached cedar shingle walls and roofs, and white trim. The interior has a combination of brick-paved and bleached oak floors and pickled cedar and painted drywall walls and ceilings. Twenty-six french doors allow for cross-ventilation and easy access from the interior to the exterior.

Other features of the house include a covered terrace at the master bedroom, an open (plan and section) skylit kitchen, a loft in one guest bedroom and a stair that doubles as a library, in addition to numerous built-ins throughout.

EAST ELEVATION

WEST ELEVATION

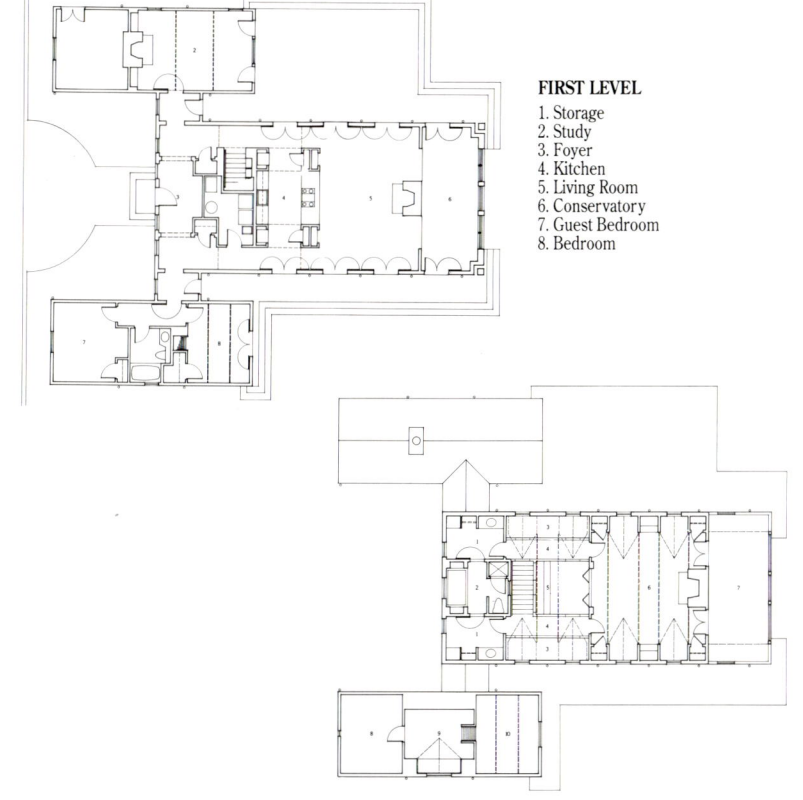

FIRST LEVEL
1. Storage
2. Study
3. Foyer
4. Kitchen
5. Living Room
6. Conservatory
7. Guest Bedroom
8. Bedroom

SECOND LEVEL
1. Dressing Room
2. Master Bathroom
3. Open to Hall Below
4. Bridge
5. Open to Kitchen Below
6. Master Bedroom
7. Terrace
8. Storage
9. Loft to Bedroom
10. Open to Bedroom

SITE PLAN

PROJECT
Walsh/Woodward residence
Edgewater, MD

ARCHITECT
Muse-Wiedemann Architects
5630 Connecticut Avenue, NW
Washington, DC 20015
Telephone (202) 966 1266

OWNER
Bob Woodward and Elsa Walsh
Washington, DC

Size and Capacity
Number of units - 1
Gross square feet - 3,000

Construction Type
New

Construction Cost
N/A

Status
Complete, 1988

Consultant
Barbara Woodward
Annapolis, MD

Contractor
Horizon Builders
Crofton, MD

Photographer: Walter Smalling

The design requirements for this house on the oceanfront walk in Venice, California, were that it engage beachfront activities while providing upper level private spaces and decks. The envelope extends to the 3-foot side setbacks and the front and rear setbacks on the 90'x28' lot with parking below the living level.

Apart from its intense social connections with the beach, the house affirms mythic connections to sea and geologic past. By using a diverging upward-sloping ceiling and a sea-related glistening black granite runway on the floor, the reversed perspective draws the ocean toward the viewer. On the ocean side, a cast-in-place concrete armature suggests bleached bones along the shore. A granite-clad monolith covered with a film of water separates the house from a public walk along the beach five feet below. When viewed from within, this water to ocean relationship expresses the spiritual connection of house to timeless place. The monolith also becomes an urban offering inviting the passerby to touch the film of water. The red steel pivot window at the end of the axis pays homage to the color of the Japanese flag, just as the granite runway within the house propels the viewer toward Japan.

The window pivots horizontally to form a 9'x13.5' high opening to the ocean. The flanking vertical slit of cast-in-place glass creates a mysterious threshold to the west as the incoming sun bombards the space with laser-like green rays. Timeless aspects of Los Angeles rather than the "glitter" are expressed: sea, stone, desert, wind rushing in the pivot window; the mystery of light entering the vertical glass slit.

Cantilevered balconies define the entry on the street side, affording protection from the rain. Throughout the interior, zones of natural light diffused through obscure glass create lateral divisions suffusing the street/entry end with soft light. A mirrored garage door acknowledges temporal Los Angeles. Upstairs, a concrete frame creates an aperture that focuses the ocean view from the bed toward the ocean. Tile stairs ascend from the master bedroom terrace to upper roof terrace "bleachers" and the deck to offer views in all directions: city lights, beach, Pacific Ocean, LAX takeoffs, Palos Verdes, Malibu, Hollywood hills. The south elevation will eventually be blocked by a house.

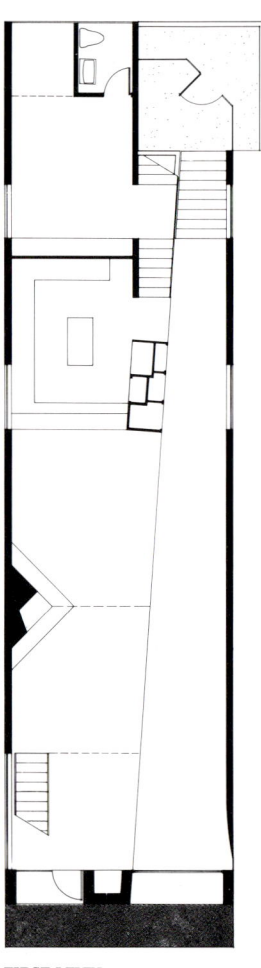

FIRST LEVEL

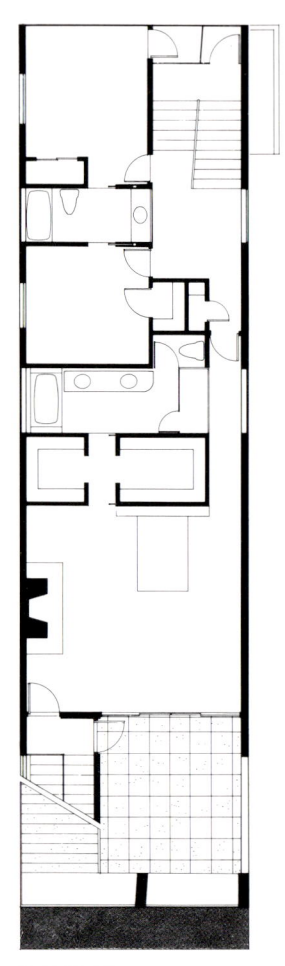

SECOND LEVEL

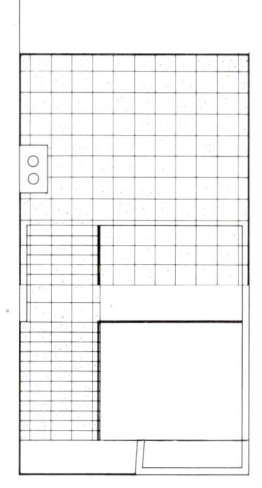

THIRD LEVEL

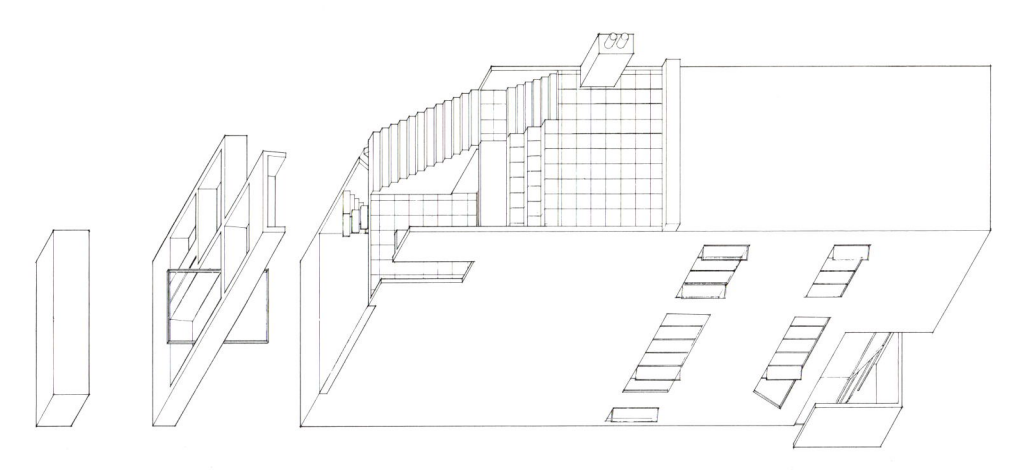

Photography: Timothy Hursley

PROJECT
Venice house
Venice Beach, CA

ARCHITECT
Antoine Predock Architect
300 12th Street NW
Albuquerque, NM 87102
Telephone (505) 843 7390

OWNER
N/A

Size and Capacity
Number of units - 1
Gross square feet - 5,030
inclusive of garage

Construction Type
New

Construction Cost
N/A

Status
Complete, June 1990

Engineer
Parker Resnick
Los Angeles, CA
Structural Engineer

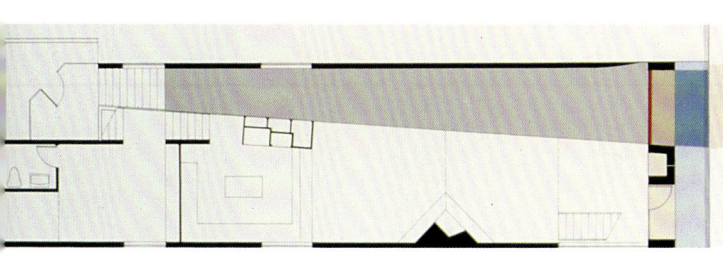

This house and studio space for two distinguished modern musicians occupies an infill lot on Potrero Hill in San Francisco. From the outside it is a seamless black object of ambiguous scale. Its odd shape is the result of acoustic requirements and planning restrictions. The interior is an open loft finished in stucco lustro, perforated steel, and zinc.

At the center of the house are a skylit rotunda and a double spiral stair, which allow daylight to penetrate to the glass block entry at the street-level garage.

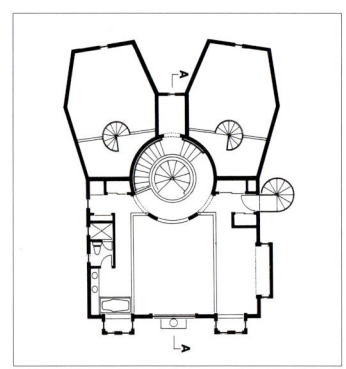

SECOND LEVEL

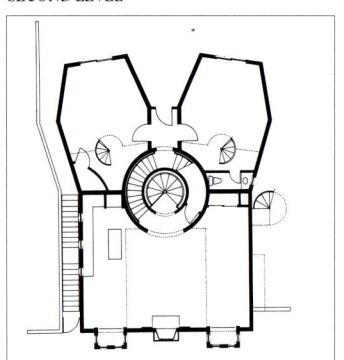

THIRD LEVEL

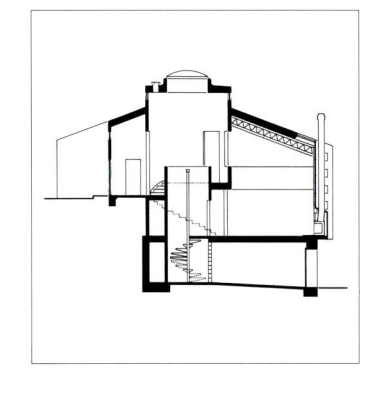

Photography: Christopher Irion

PROJECT
House for two musicians
San Francisco, CA

ARCHITECT
Solomon, Inc.
(Daniel Solomon Design Principal, Stuart Wright and Vladimir Frank, Project Architects)
84 Vandewater Street
San Francisco, CA
Telephone (415) 397 9190

OWNER
Pat Gleeson/Jean Jeanrenaud
San Francisco, CA

Size and Capacity
Number of units - 1
Gross square feet - 2,560

Construction Type
New

Construction Cost
N/A

Status
Complete

Engineers
Shapiro Okino Hom & Associates
San Francisco, CA
Structural Engineer

F.W. Associates
San Francisco, CA
Mechanical and Electrical Engineers

Consultants
Solomon, Inc.
San Francisco, CA
Landscape Architect

Terry Hunziker
Seattle, WA
Interiors

John Storyk
Acoustical

Contractor
Praxis Construction
St. Helena, CA

This house was designed by and for an architect and his wife, a graphic designer and avid gardener. Since moving to Southern California they had imagined building a courtyard house in close partnership with the landscape and climate. Several years of searching yielded the only buildable lot in budget, a hillside lot of 100'x600' bordered by a dry creek on the west.

Coastal Commission requirements prevented building within 50 feet of this edge and Fire Department access required 18 feet on the eastern edge. The resultant 32'x600' buildable area had dissuaded other buyers but challenged and intrigued them.

The house evolved from the constraints and pleasures of the site. From east to west the house unfolds as layers of habitation: From carefully proportioned rooms to a sunny gallery broad enough for seating and dining, to a stepping street, on to a set of pergolas that function as garden rooms of varying character, then to cultivated gardens and finally to the streambed and uncultivated chaparral. The north-south transformations are equally important. The lot is graced with a serene due north mountain view and a complementary view south to the ocean. Movement along this axis connects a series of outside courtyards. One drives toward the mountain, along the eastern wall of the house, to the parking court and then begins to move through a sequence of courts heading back toward the ocean view. Inside, the gallery and library emphasize the mountain-to-ocean axis. Outside, the terraced street links a series of courts.

The house closely responds to concerns of proportion and light. Its extruded shape was both economical and reminiscent of farmhouses in California and other warm coastal climates. Its tower and library reach for the ocean and mountain views that animate the house. Despite the tight footprint, the vertical movement of the house gives every room multiple views and breezes. The hearths focus life around the warm center of the house in winter. A sleeping porch, gallery, street, courts, and pergolas allow for connections to the benign climate and landscape much of the year.

The richness of experience derives from the overlay of the east-west transformation (formal rooms to native landscape) with the north-south, mountain-to-sea movement. The interplay of geometry, space, orientation, and landscape creates a place that is at once serene and full of unfolding experiences.

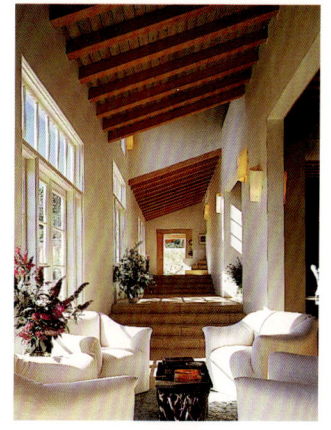

Photography: Timothy Hursley

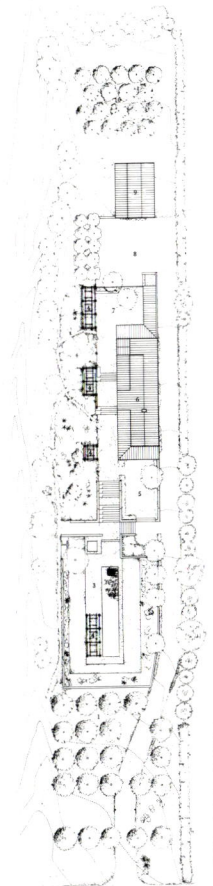

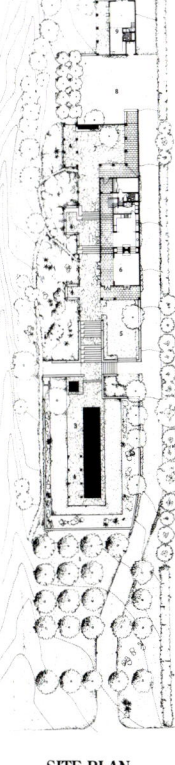

PROJECT
Yudell/Beebe House
Malibu, CA

ARCHITECT
Buzz Yudell
933 Pico Boulevard
Santa Monica, CA 90405
Telephone (213) 450 1400

OWNER
Buzz Yudell and Tina Beebe
Malibu, CA

Size and Capacity
Number of units - 1
Gross square feet - 3,400

Construction Type
New

Construction Cost
N/A

Status
Complete, Spring 1989

Engineer
CASA Engineers
Canoga Park, CA
Structural Engineer

Consultant
Tina Beebe
Malibu, CA
Landscape Designer

Contractor
Bruce Brown Construction
Santa Monica, CA

1. Olive Grove
2. Pool
3. Pool Court
4. Pergola
5. Rose Court
6. House
7. Entry Court
8. Parking Court
9. Studio/Guest
10. Citrus Orchard

ROOF PLAN   SITE PLAN

49

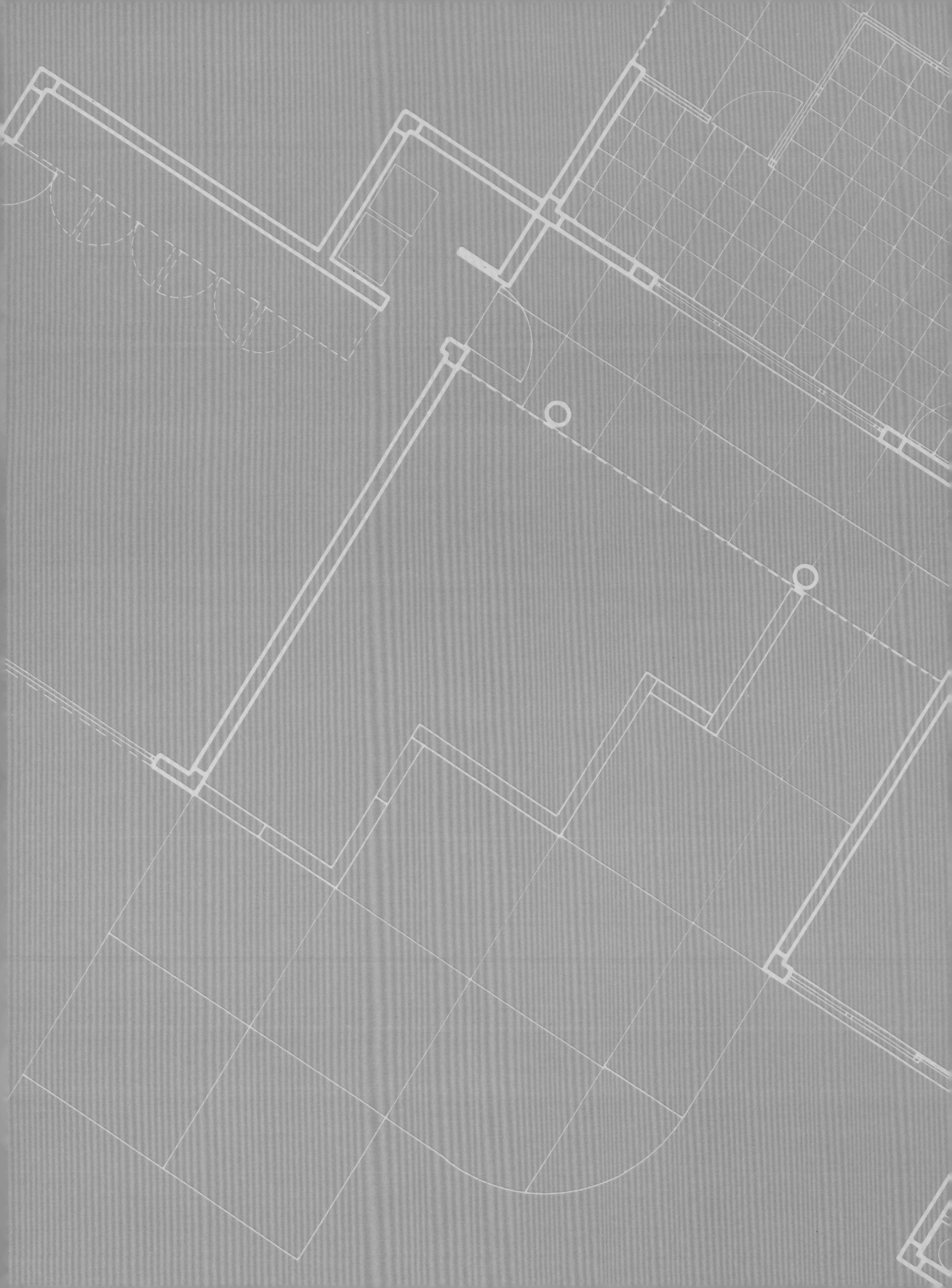

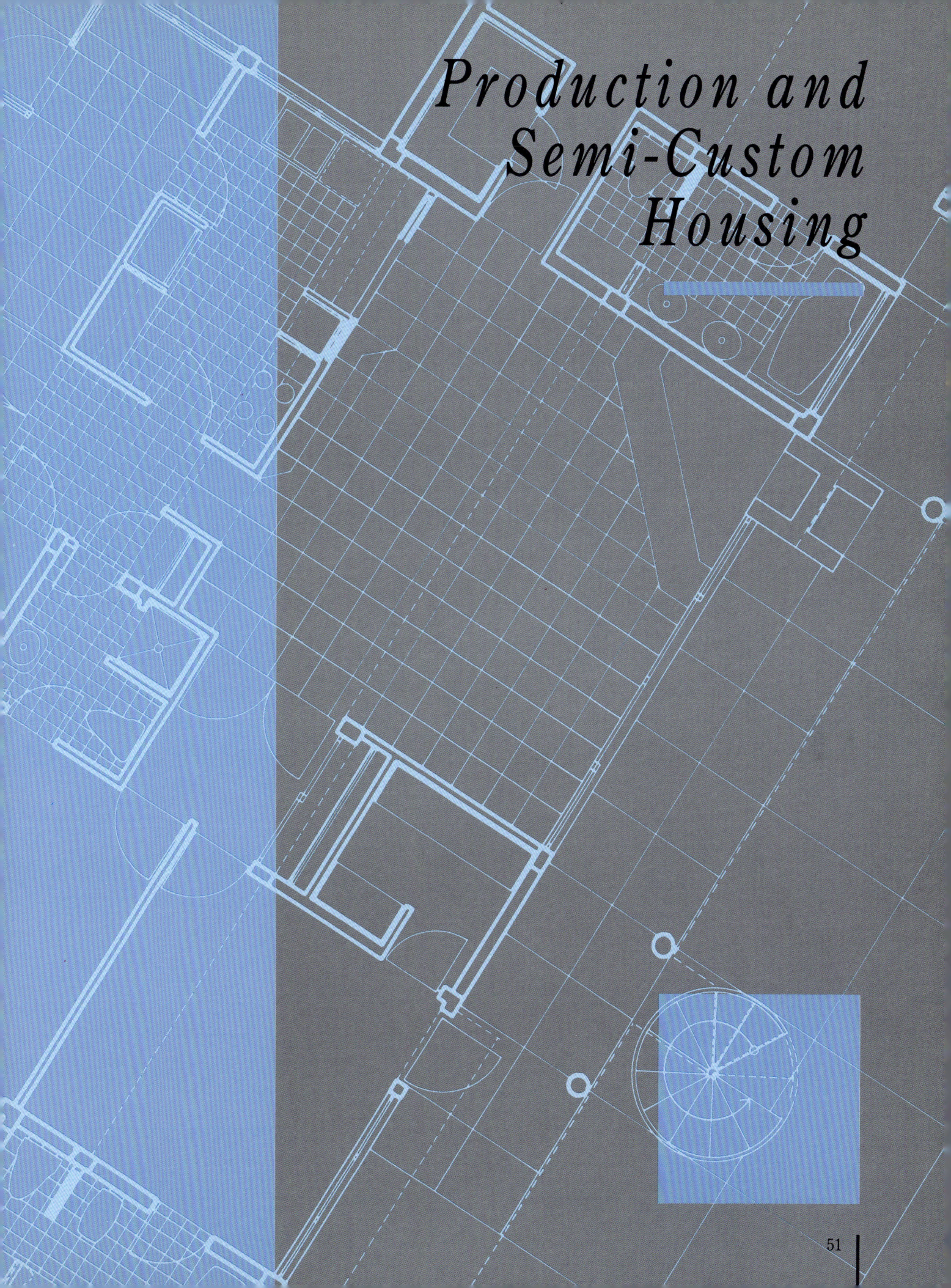

Production and Semi-Custom Housing

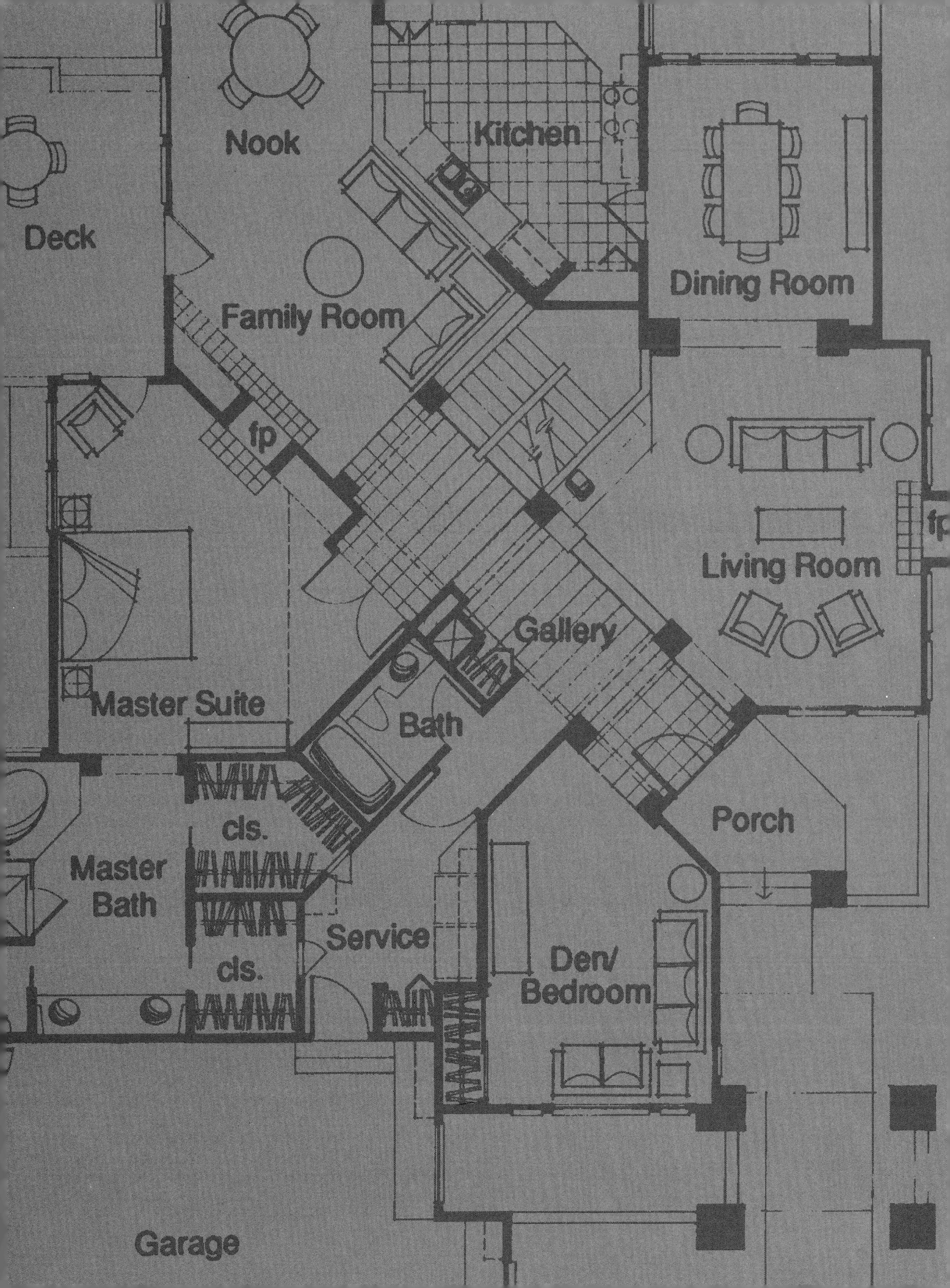

- Deck
- Nook
- Kitchen
- Dining Room
- Family Room
- fp
- Living Room
- Gallery
- Master Suite
- Bath
- Porch
- cls.
- Master Bath
- cls.
- Service
- Den/Bedroom
- Garage
- fp

Production and Semi-Custom Housing

In the 1980s, production housing and the variety of "semi-custom" homes many smaller volume builders offer, demonstrated a giant step forward from the barracks-look response to the huge post–World War II housing demand. In the 1990s, more important changes will occur, but within a considerably less frenzied atmosphere than the boom and bust cycles of the past 40 years.

The economy will be slower paced in the 1990s – with fewer and less severe peaks and plunges – yet the housing market will be sturdy and dependable, thanks to the continuing ascent of the Baby Boomers into their peak wage-earning years. Because the beginning and end of the Baby Boom bulge stretches over nearly 20 years, we'll feel the impact gradually and continually in a variety of market segments.

"Good" and "bad" housing markets are thus less likely to have national parameters in the 1990s than in the past, and "hot" and troubled markets are more likely to reflect local and regional conditions than a national picture.

While there's not likely to be a national housing market that's all good or all bad, a number of trends in housing will be reflected fairly consistently nationally. The price of housing will continue to increase, with land and development costs as the primary culprits. That means the first owned home will be harder and harder to come by.

Since owning a home will require a larger and larger initial investment – yet ownership is likely to become less of a "sure thing" in terms of investment appreciation – rentals may well become an alternative of *choice*, not just necessity, in more and more markets.

Whether owned or rented, homes will offer more traditional styling, with distinctive regional emphases. Interior detailing will reflect the exterior style, rather than being a separate entity as we've seen during much of the 1980s. That doesn't mean interiors will be dark and chopped-up into many small rooms like older versions of "traditional." To the contrary, interiors will be opened-up, offering volume and diagonal views, and emphasizing indoor-outdoor relationships.

Shared and multi-use spaces will be attractive to many homebuyers – but successful designs for these rooms will also make sense, and not appear contrived. The home office is more likely to be a requirement than an option, as the computer continues to expand the meaning of "going to work." While family rooms or great rooms will continue to be high on the list of expectations, master suites as adult retreats are likely to vie for some of the space formerly allotted to family areas.

Although buyers in some areas of the country will continue to accept attached houses (part of the regionalism influence), more are likely to turn their backs on builders' attached experiments of the early and mid-1980s in favour of their first love – detached, single-family homes.

Creative site planning will be a prerequisite for contending with ever-increasing land and development costs in the delivery of these desired single-family homes to a range of market segments – and for changing the definition of "conventional" lot size. Using innovative planning concepts, acceptable single-family densities are likely to be in the range of six units to the acre. For those buyers priced out of the market at these "lower" densities, acceptable alternatives to attached products may well be in the range of 8 to 12 units to the acre.

The most sought-after production and semi-custom homes in the 1990s will be located in planned communities. Good planned communities will enable the most successful implementation of small lot concepts; will enhance home investment prospects; and will provide the amenities and the conveniences that evoke "lifestyle" in buyers' minds instead of "shelter." Golf courses, water, equestrian centers and other simpler community themes will be the focal points of these successful planned communities. They will also require the thoughtful integration of architecture, planning, landscape design, and engineering.

R. Bruce Downing, AIA

Merit

This cottage project was intended to provide a low-cost, low-maintenance, attractive model for new public housing for the homeless that could be built using unskilled, volunteer labor. The cottages were designed using the small freedmen cottages, built in the late 19th century, as a case study. The floor plan is designed as a module, allowing the cottages to be stacked on top of one another or side by side in any quantity desired. The 352 square foot cottage has a combined bedroom, living space, bathroom, efficiency kitchen, and loft for storage or additional sleeping space. Mayor Riley's Subcommittee on Housing has not designed a "roof only" solution. The people who occupy these houses will continue to receive case management support for up to a year from social workers.

This project was developed through the cooperative efforts of several organizations without any help from federal sources. The Charleston Housing Authority donated the land and funding for one house; the city parks department provided fill and labor to prepare the site; Charleston Habitat for Humanity provided the labor for the foundations, and finish and trim work; a Donor-Advised Fund of the Trident Community Foundation and St. Phillip's Episcopal Church provided the funding for two additional houses.

After the residents and their social workers agree they are ready to move to the next step, they will be placed in the city's transitional housing. From this point, the residents can eventually move into a permanent home. The one common denominator for all the homeless is the need for a roof over their heads; however, there are often other needs, including a bridge back to self-sufficiency. This cottage project provides that bridge – a place where people can "catch their breath" and begin to regain confidence and dignity.

The Charleston Cottages won a 1991 Honor Award from the American Institute of Architects.

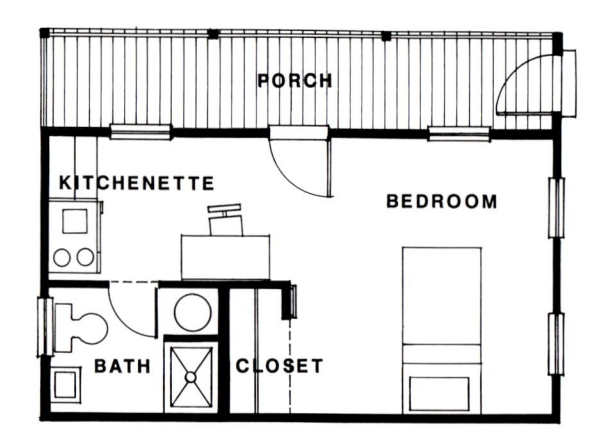

Photography: Chris Schmitt & Associates, Inc.

PROJECT
Charleston Cottages
Charleston, SC

ARCHITECTS
Chris Schmitt & Associates, Inc.
113 Wappoo Creek Drive
Suite 6
Charleston, SC 29412
Telephone (803) 795 8752

Project Architect
Christopher A. Rose, AIA

OWNER
The Housing Authority
of the city of Charleston
Charleston, SC

Project Type
Production, housing for homeless

Size and Capacity
Number of units - 3
Gross square feet - 352
Ratio of gross: Net - 1:1
Density of gross: Net - 6 u/a

Construction Type
New

Construction Cost
$34 per square foot

Status
Complete, June 1989

Engineers
Insul-Kor of Florida, Inc.
Hilliard, FL
Structural Engineer

Construction Technologies, Inc.
Summerville, SC
Mechanical and Electrical Engineer

Consultants
Steve Livingston – city of Charleston
Parks & Recreation
Charleston, SC
Landscape Architect

Contractor
Southeastern Construction
and Volunteers
Mt. Pleasant, SC

Merit

The developer of this 24-unit cottage project located near the beach in a premier coastal resort community did not want to follow the usual formula of designing quasi-contemporary housing units with rough-sawn cypress siding stained environmental gray. Instead, he wanted to make a statement that reflected the architectural heritage of southeastern summer beach communities. The model the developer and architect chose for this project was the older beach communities on the islands directly adjacent to this resort community. There the summer homes constructed at the turn of the century or earlier featured open informal floor plans, generous front and rear porches, metal roofs, large double-hung windows for light and ventilation, traditional clapboard siding, and high ceilings with ceiling fans throughout to augment the natural ventilation and cooling.

These 24 homes were designed and constructed using simple, direct wood frame construction that is commensurate with the technology and building materials available as well as being consistent with the type of construction historically used for beach homes in the area. The centerpiece of the neighborhood is a landscaped area featuring a croquet lawn and a trellised gazebo that can be used for cookouts and other social functions. The entire neighborhood is tied together through the use of white picket fences and pastel paint colors that reinforce the architectural concept.

contd.

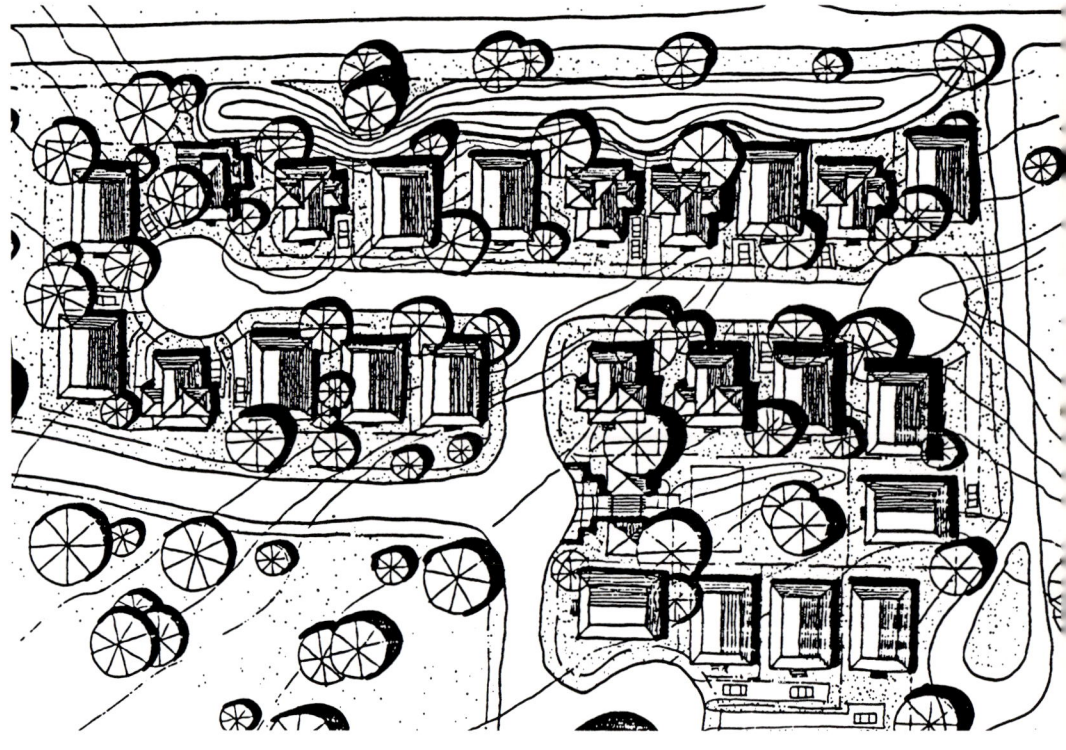

SITE PLAN

PROJECT
Seaside at Wild Dunes
Wild Dunes Beach & Racquet Club
Isle of Palms, SC

ARCHITECT
Chris Schmitt & Associates, Inc.
113 Wappoo Creek Drive
Suite 6
Charleston, SC 29412
Telephone (803) 795 8752

OWNER
The Bennett Hofford Company
Charleston, SC

Project Type
Single-family multiple,
second home, resort

Size and Capacity
Number of units - 24
Gross square feet - 48,856
Ratio of gross: Net - 1:1
Density of gross: Net - 5.1 u/a

Construction Type
New

Construction Cost
$57.00 per square foot

Status
Complete, September 1988

Engineers
T. G. Padgett & Associates
Charleston, SC
Structural Engineer

Engineering Associates
Charleston, SC
Mechanical and Electrical Engineer

Thomas & Hutton
Engineering Company
Mount Pleasant, SC
Civil Engineers

Consultant
Chris Schmitt & Associates, Inc.
Charleston, SC

Contractor
The Bennett Hofford Company
Charleston, SC

Photography: Creative Sources Photography

57

The unit mix consists of three types ranging from 1,700 to 2,300 square feet and from one to three stories. This variety allows the project to appeal to a wide range of buyers. The interiors feature 10-foot ceilings with fans, wood floors, and large double-hung windows and beaded wood paneling in the major living spaces.

The site plan was determined by an existing plat for these lots, which the project developer purchased from the resort community. The intent was to create a strong sense of place, and the architecture and materials are unmistakably associated with the coastal lifestyle in this part of the country. This project is truly a family place at the beach.

SEA WATCH FIRST LEVEL

SEA WATCH SECOND LEVEL

SEA WATCH THIRD LEVEL

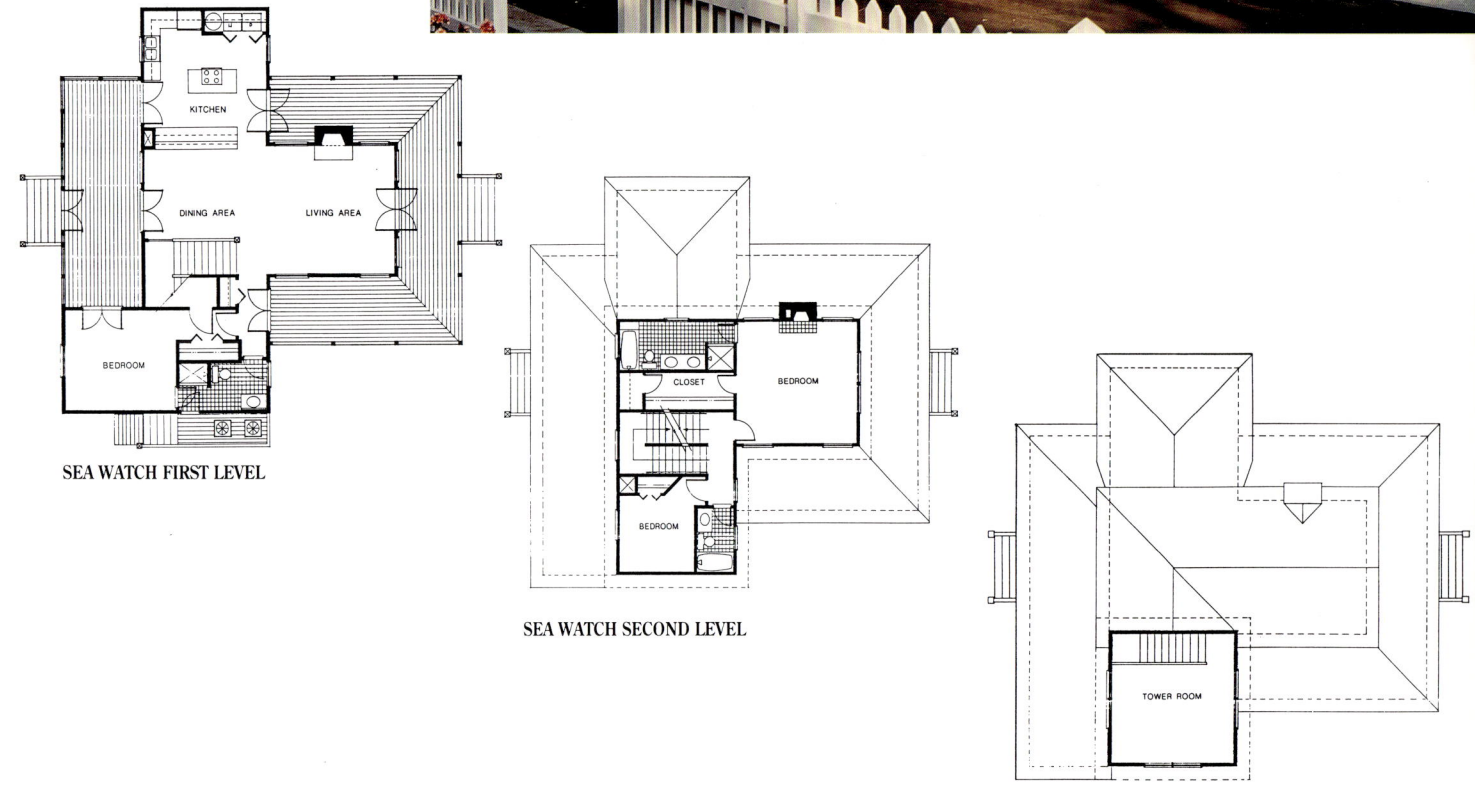

Photography: Creative Sources Photography

59

Mention

From security to lighting to privacy, the design of active retirement housing such as Lakeshire requires a perspective that is both practical and compassionate. Far from the masterful illusions of space and glamour architects often create for the young move-up market, retirement housing must match the mind-set of the aging adult who is above all realistic about physical and financial restraints.

One of the most critical design challenges in this market was eliminating or reducing stairs. This goal was made even more difficult by the hilly terrain that is often common in scenic golf course communities.

Inside, the architecture responds to very clear demands expressed by this market. Room for memories is designed in since these buyers bring a lifetime of furniture, accessories, and other collectibles that must be accommodated. Still, retirees are very alert to wasted space such as volume ceilings and high shelving, which they judge to be impractical to heat and impossible to clean.

Traditionalism had to prevail in the design and arrangement of rooms. Based on research, a wish list for a retirement unit in this region reads like a housing formula from the '50s: separate living and dining rooms, a TV room, a large master bedroom with a long wall for the seven-foot dresser, a guest room, and a big kitchen with oversized breakfast room. If there was square footage left over, a family room was added.

Photography: Creative Vision

SITE PLAN

PROJECT
Lakeshire
Walnut Creek, CA

ARCHITECT
EDI Architecture/Planning
333 Broadway
San Francisco, CA 94133
Telephone (415) 362 2880

OWNER
UDC Homes
Pleasanton, CA

Project Type
Single-family attached, duplex and triplex

Size and Capacity
Number of units - 37
Density of gross: Net - 3.78 u/a

Construction Type
New

Construction Cost
$6.5 million

Status
Complete, May 1989

Engineers
Lee Mason & Associates
Lafayette, CA
Structural Engineer

Steadman & Associates
Walnut Creek, CA
Civil Engineer

Consultants
Anthony Guzzardo Associates, Inc.
San Francisco, CA
Landscape Architect

Interior Resources Design
Alamo, CA
Interior Design

Contractor
UDC Homes
Pleasanton, CA

61

Nestled against a golf course and among several landscaped ponds, The Villas at Stonehaven offer handsome surroundings and a carefree lifestyle to move-down and second-home buyers seeking luxury as well as convenience in smaller, detached single-family homes. Located in Highland Springs, an upscale, master-planned community, The Villas patio homes offer five floor plans, all with luxurious master suites and distinctive interior design features, such as columns, half-walls, and sculptured dry-wall lights. Exteriors feature low-maintenance stucco, native stone, and tile roofs. Custom-made outdoor lights and flashings are copper. Inside and out, finishes and architectural detailing reflect the quality levels generally expected in custom homes, which are the only other housing choices currently available in the community.

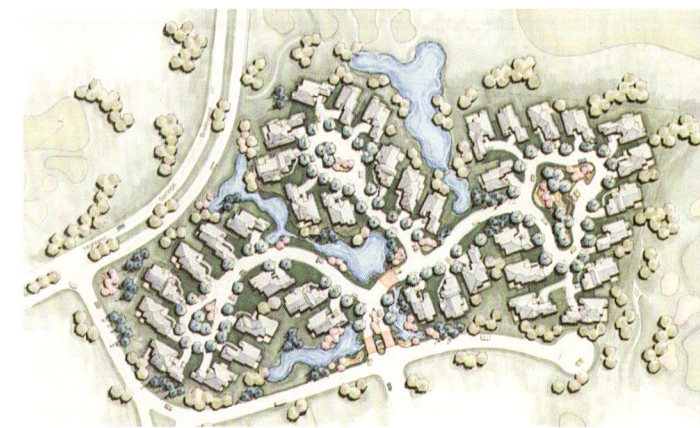

SITE PLAN

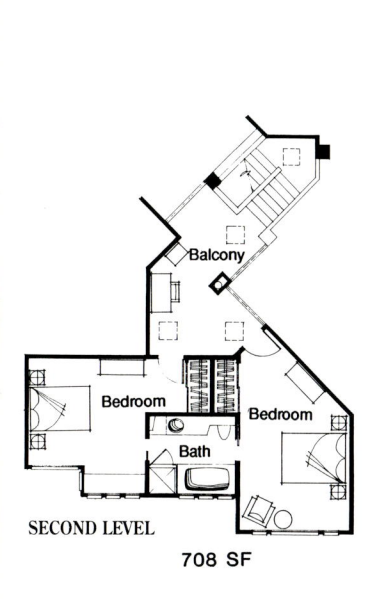

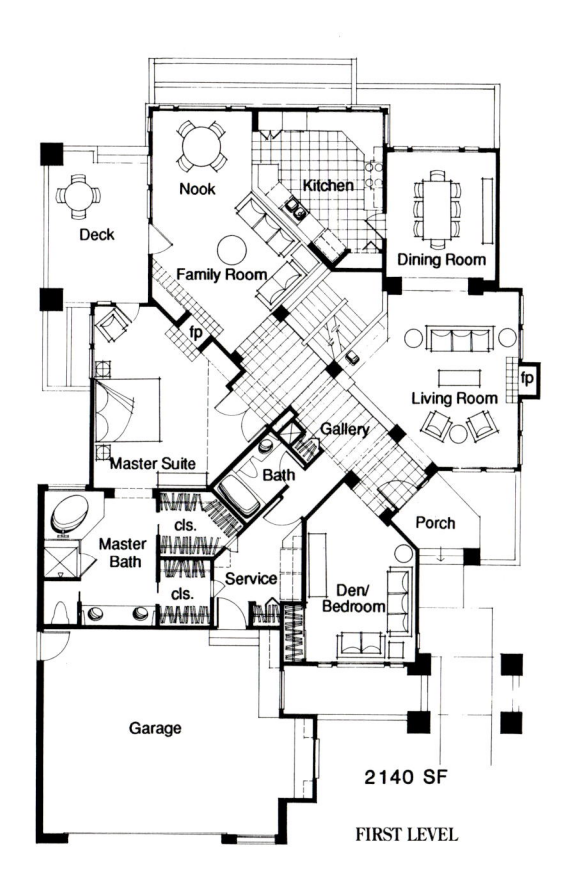

PROJECT
The Villas at Stonehaven
Highland Springs Country Club
Springfield, MO

ARCHITECT
Downing, Thorpe & James, Inc.
1881 9th Street
Suite 103
Boulder, CO 80302
Telephone (303) 443 7533

OWNER
Mr. John Q. Hammons
Springfield, MO

Project Type
Single-family production

Size and Capacity
Number of units - 39
Units range from 1,510 to 2,848 square feet
Density of gross: Net - 3.9 u/a

Construction Type
Cluster homes
New

Construction Cost
N/A

Status
Complete, July 1990

Engineer
Gebau Engineering
Boulder, CO
Structural Engineer

Photography: Rockafellow Photography

63

Lee's Orchard, a residential project at the south end of San Francisco Bay at the edge of Santa Clara Valley, reinstates aspects of the historic landscape of the Milpitas Hills. In place of conventional suburban landscaping, a newly planted orchard of a thousand olive trees serves as the principal feature of the developed portion of the property. Roads and driveways align with the grid of trees. One enters the site between windrows of poplar trees, on a road that loops around a central open space with a recreation building, swimming pool, and storage for orchard equipment.

Thirteen single-family houses are placed in clearings within the geometry of the orchard. The house designs are based on traditional California farmhouses with porches, picket rails, and clapboard siding. The interiors of all house types offer spatial complexity, double height interior volumes, views, elaborate kitchens, fancy bath suites, and all the amenities of production houses.

The floor plans of the four house types have simple configurations. The most repeated house type has a 2-story porch wrapped around its rectangular floor plan. Another house type, derived from the "dogtrot" house, has a simple square plan with an internal 2-story skylit outdoor space. A third house type, L-shaped in plan, has a 2-story opening similar to a barn at its entry and a bridge that connects the main living portion with the bedroom wing. The only single story plan type takes its cues from the conventional ranch house with its U-shaped plan and entrance courtyard.

Photograpy and model: Peter Xiques

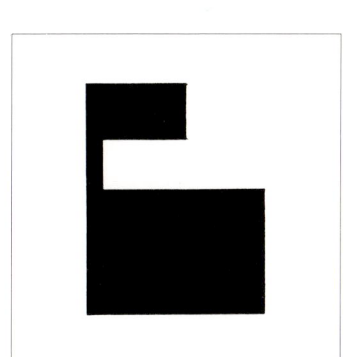

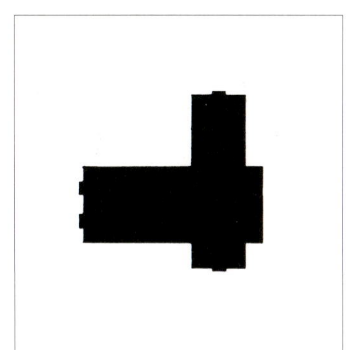

PROJECT
Lee's Orchard
Milpitas, CA

ARCHITECT
Solomon, Inc.
(Daniel Solomon & Kathryn Clarke,
Co-design Principals)
84 Vandewater Street
San Francisco, CA
Telephone (415) 397 9190

OWNER
Jon Schink
Palo Alto, CA

Project Type
Single-family multiple, second home

Size and Capacity
Number of units - 13
Units range from 3,800 to 4,400 square feet

Construction Type
New

Construction Cost
N/A

Status
Partly complete

Engineers
Structural Design Engineers
San Francisco, CA
Structural Engineer

HMH, Inc.
San Jose, CA
Civil Engineer

Consultants
Gary Strang
Solomon, Inc.
San Francisco, CA
Landscape Architect

Barbara Stauffacher Solomon
San Francisco, CA
Conceptual Landscape Design

Hydro-Geo Consultants, Inc.
Palo Alto, CA
Geotechnical Consultant

Contractor
Standford Building Group
Palo Alto, CA

65

This development group's six shingle-style houses sit along a newly created cul-de-sac in one of Boston's affluent bedroom communities. A consistent vocabulary is established employing shingled walls and roofs, bays, turrets, and covered porches that allows each individual house to vary considerably from its neighbor with regard to massing and floor plan, while maintaining an integrity to the development. Each 3,500 square foot house is designed specially for its location on the street, taking advantage of considerable topographical variety in the site as well as sight lines and real or implied arcs. The assemblage is designed to appeal to a variety of homeowners seeking to accommodate contemporary lifestyles in a traditional architectural environment.

Photography: William Choi

SITE PLAN

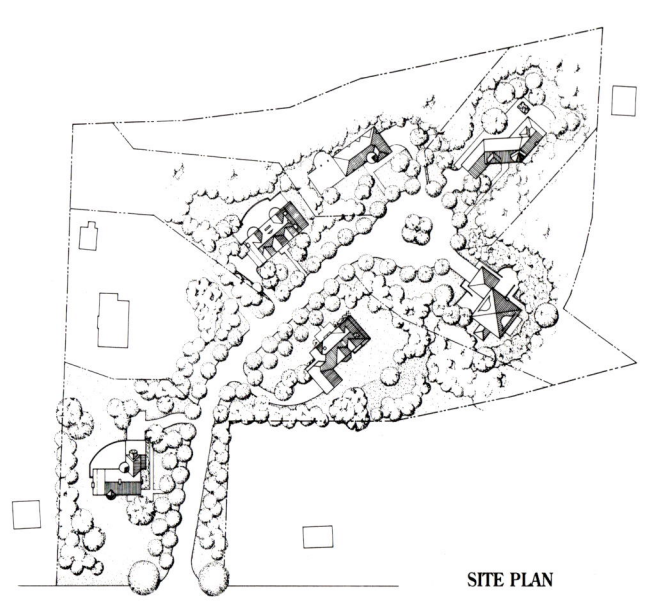

Photography: Cymie Payne

HOUSE 4   HOUSE 6

EAST ELEVATION   EAST ELEVATION

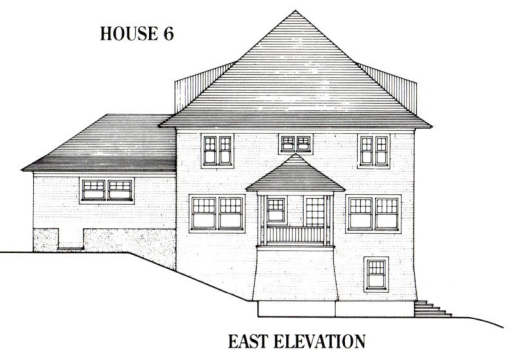

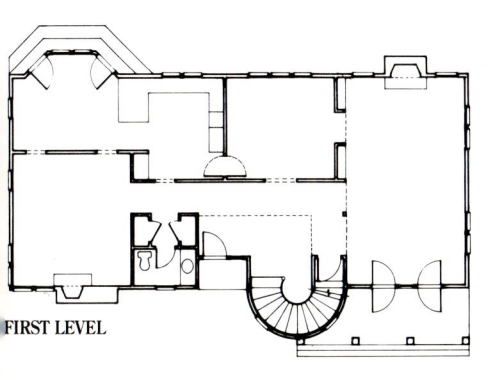

FIRST LEVEL

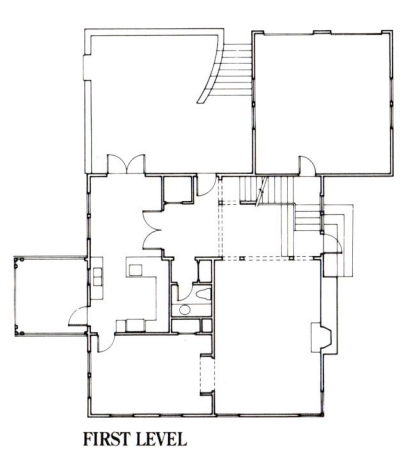

FIRST LEVEL

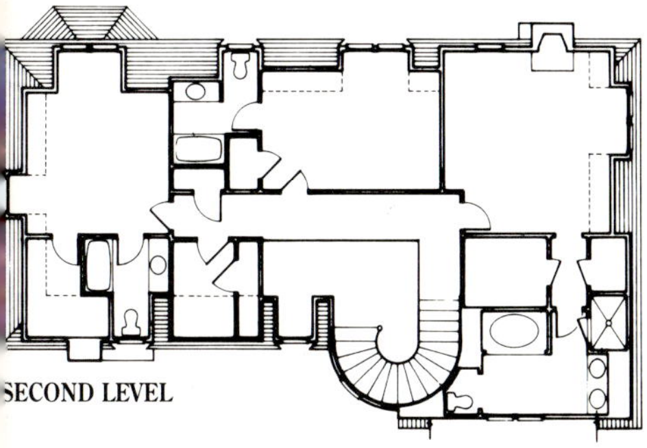

SECOND LEVEL

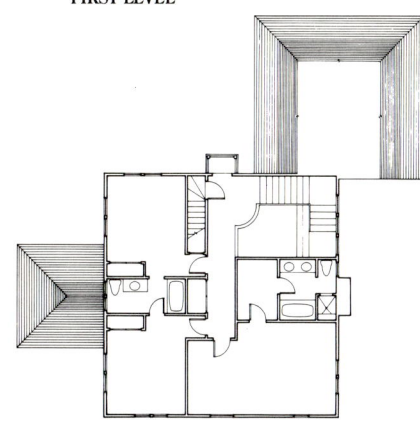

SECOND LEVEL

Photography: William Choi

Photography: William Choi    Photography: William Choi

PROJECT
The Hamptons
Lexington, MA

ARCHITECT
Robert A.M. Stern Architects
211 West 61st Street
New York, NY 10023
Telephone (212) 246 1980

OWNER
Boyd/Smith Inc.
Boston, MA

Project Type
Single-family multiple

Size and Capacity
Number of units - 6
Gross square feet - 3,200
Density of gross: Net - 1 u/a

Construction Type
New

Construction Cost
$600,000 per unit

Status
Complete, 1987

Engineer
Robert Silman & Associates
New York, NY
Structural Engineer

Consultant
The SWA Group
Boston, MA
Landscape Architect

67

Breckenridge is a community of 43 single-family detached homes planned and designed to address the affordable housing market. By offering detached homes in the $59,000 – $79,000 range, the homebuilder is providing much needed housing for the community at affordable prices.

In order to provide the cost savings needed to build in this price range, a high-density prototype was developed for 36' wide lots yielding over 7 units to the acre. The styling of the homes resembles the bungalow era "shotgun" or narrow home built extensively in the area earlier in the century. A center entry door allows the living and dining rooms and kitchen to face the rear of the lot with a view to the private patio.

The traditional but compact exteriors of these homes possess all the detailing necessary for an appealing neighborhood streetscape. The interior plans are designed to address the diversity of the affordable market. First-time buyers are offered open designs with vaulted ceilings and optional fireplaces and skylights. The rear and side orientation of double glass sliding doors extends the living environment and provides a sense of "quiet privacy" within the security of a neighborhood served by a community association.

Photography: James W. Wentling

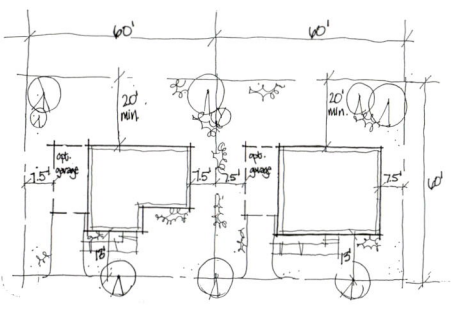

TYPICAL WIDE LOT LAYOUT

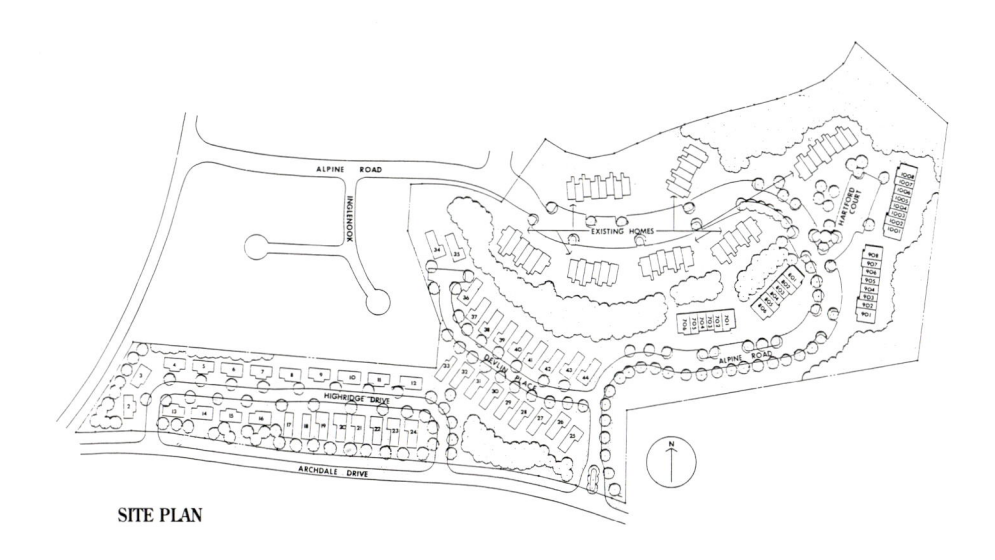

SITE PLAN

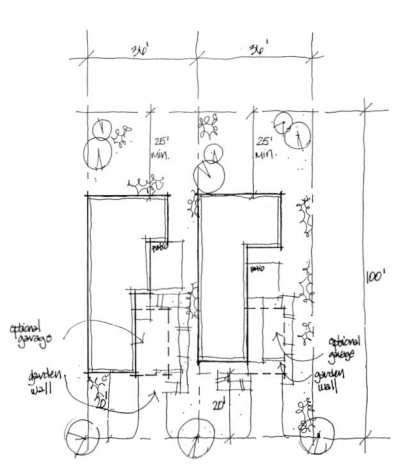

TYPICAL NARROW LOT LAYOUT

PROJECT
Breckenridge
Durham, NC

ARCHITECT
James Wentling/Architects
200 South Broad Street
Suite 900
Philadelphia, PA 19102
Telephone (215) 735 0038

OWNER
Cimarron Homes Inc.
Durham, NC

Project Type
Single-family production

Size and Capacity
Number of units - 43
Density of gross: Net - 7.17 u/a

Construction Type
New

Construction Cost
$3.18 million

Status
90% complete, Fall 1991

Engineer
Post Associates
Durham, NC
Civil Engineer

Contractor
Cimarron Homes Inc.
Durham, NC

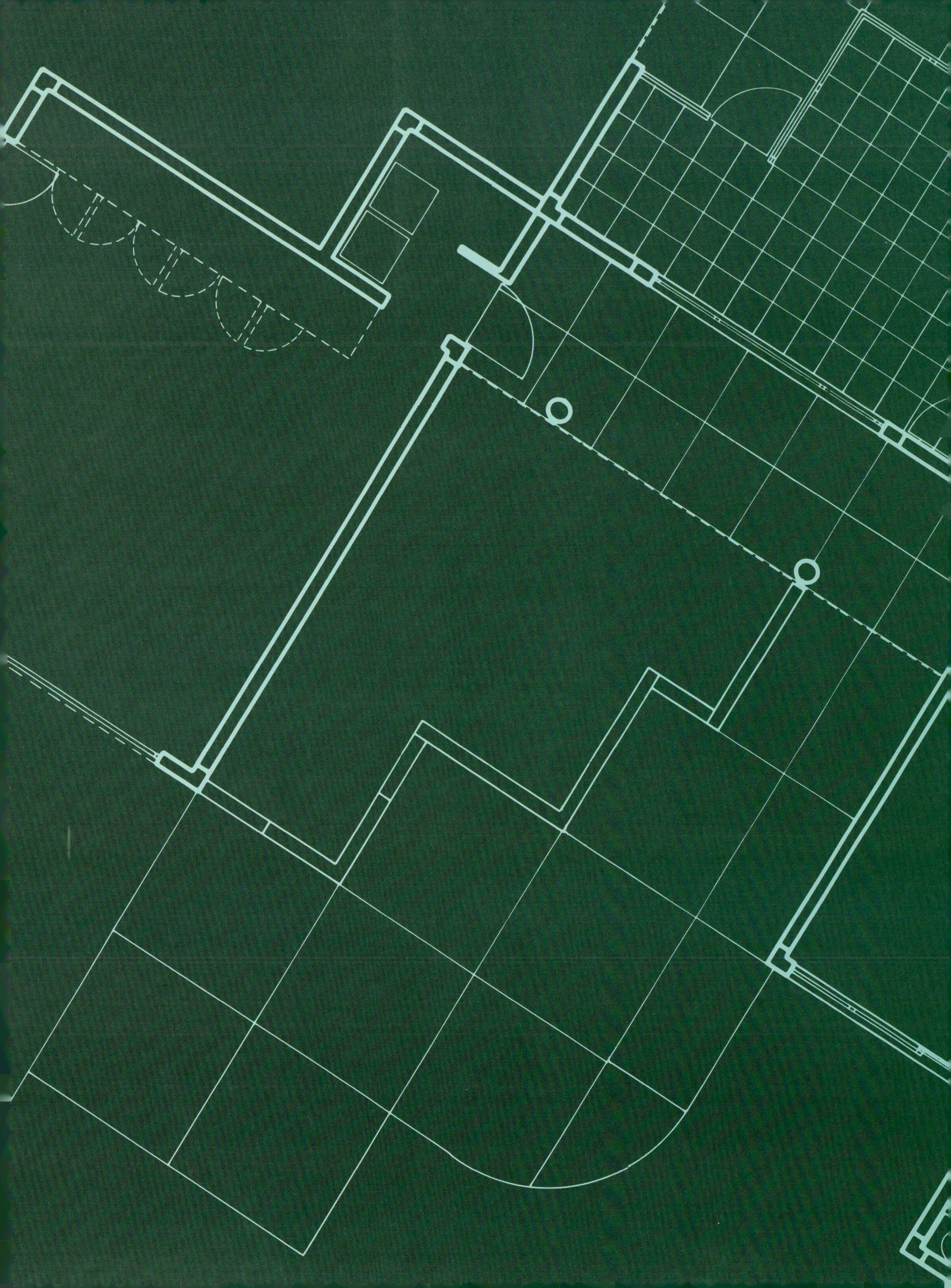

Multi-Family Housing

UNIT TYPE D

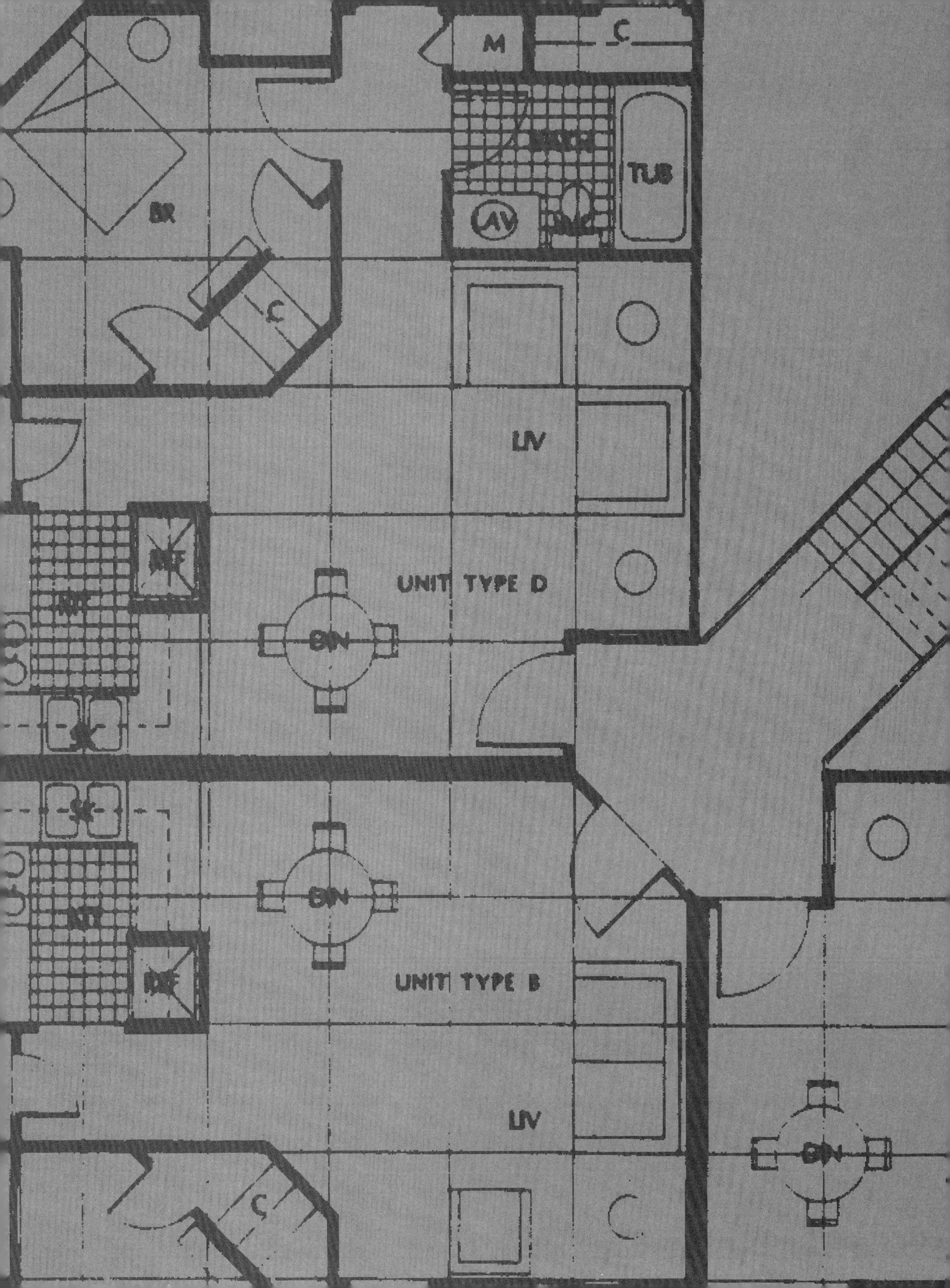

UNIT TYPE B

Multi-Family Housing

Historically a popular form of housing in cities, attached dwellings have been considered somewhat out of place in the suburban and rural American landscape. In the boom in housing construction that followed World War II, their role was primarily in rental programs and other situations where higher density and smaller square footage made economic sense.

Nevertheless, multi-family housing generally accounts for a major segment of the U.S. housing market – up to one-third of all new housing production – and its consumers have sound reasons for their preference, including shared maintenance of exteriors and common areas and the security afforded by higher density. Recently the use of attached housing has expanded to programs for a wider range of market profiles. In addition to renters and first-time buyers, today's multi-family markets include singles of varying age and income, single parents, empty-nesters, and retirees. Luxury communities consisting of attached housing oriented toward golf or other amenities have also grown in number and popularity in many geographic areas.

The marketing objective of instilling more immediate and long-term value through features that appeal to this wider range of buyer and renter profiles has made multi-family housing comparable to detached single-family production housing in terms of design attention. Multi-family housing still involves more compromises for the designer than detached housing, however. These are associated with such considerations as common walls and noise transmission, parking and access to units, small square footage, floor plan limitations, and location of mechanical cores, decks, and patio areas for stacked living quarters. Management of these constraints continues to require imagination and careful thought from architects.

James W. Wentling, AIA

Excellence

The site of Brookline's former Free Hospital for Women has been converted into "The Park." Composed of 71 unique luxury apartments and 16 new town house condominiums, The Park involved the restoration of five Victorian buildings, including the former nurses' residence and boiler house, and construction of 16 new luxury town houses. The 5-acre site is situated on Frederick Law Olmsted's "Emerald Necklace" and has a true park setting.

The exteriors of the turn-of-the-century hospital buildings were unchanged; the fenestration was kept as originally designed, with the existing windows refurbished as necessary. The interiors of the buildings were completely gutted, but conversion into contemporary one-, two-, and three-bedroom apartment units included the restoration of many fine original details. Interior details such as marble foyers, tile mosaics, leaded glass windows, and wooden trusses were maintained, resulting in unique floor plans throughout.

A major design challenge was to integrate the new town houses with the existing historic environment. Borrowing forms and detailing from the hospital and neighborhood structures, a design was derived that incorporates the mansard roofs, stepped facades, yellow masonry, and green shingles of the old into the new. These two- and three-bedroom town houses are built over a grade level, and an enclosed parking garage providing two spaces for each owner.

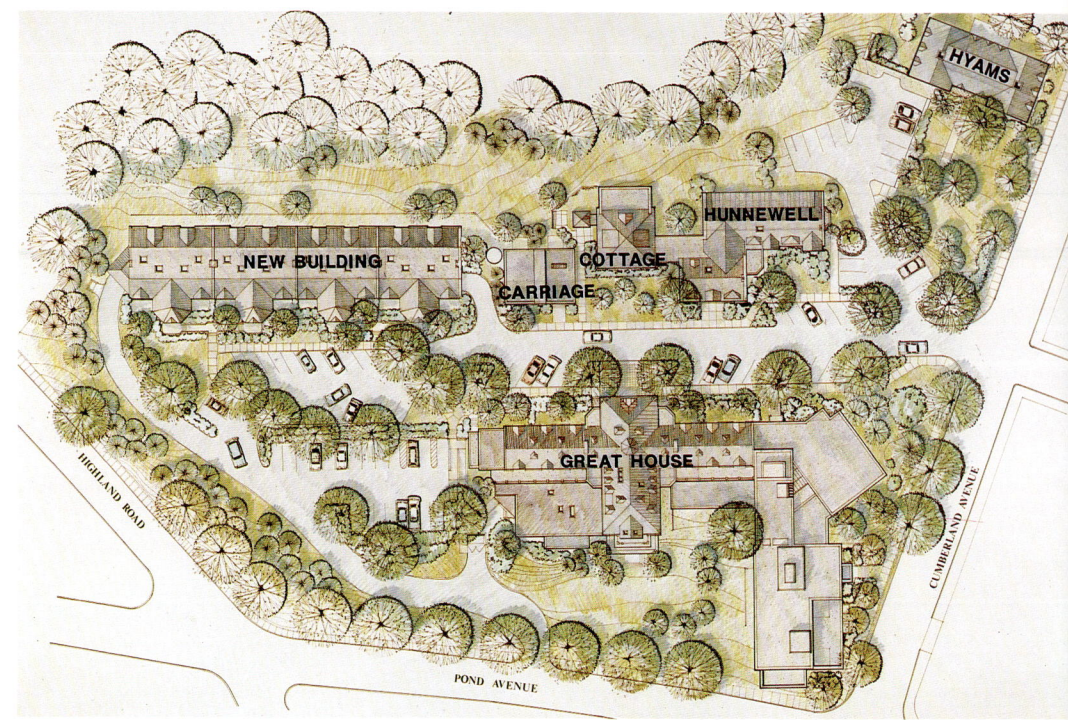

contd.

Photography: Nick Wheeler

THE HYAMS SECOND LEVEL

THE HYAMS GROUND LEVEL

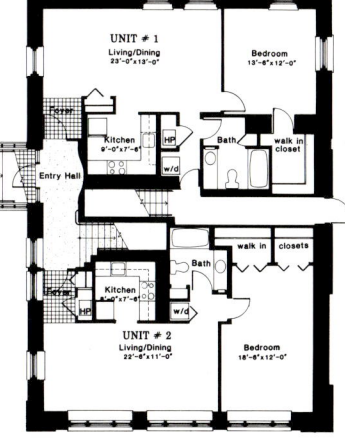

THE COTTAGE GROUND LEVEL

PROJECT
The Park
Brookline, MA

ARCHITECT
CBT/Childs Bertman Tseckares
& Casendino Inc.
306 Dartmouth Street
Boston, MA 02116
Telephone (617) 262 4354

OWNER
Myerson/Allen & Co.
Boston, MA

Size and Capacity
Number of units -
16 new, 71 renovated
Gross square feet -
101,000 new, 19,130 renovated

Construction Type
20% new, 80% renovation

Construction Cost
$21.4 million

Status
Complete, May 1987

Engineers
The Rona Associates
Boston, MA
Structural Engineer

Panitsas/Zade Associates
Boston, MA
Mechanical Engineer

Vincent D. Iorio
Boston, MA
Electrical Engineer

Consultant
CBT/Childs Bertman Tseckares
& Casendino Inc.
Boston, MA
Landscape Architect

Contractor
E. A. Gralia Construction Co. Inc.
E. Longmeadow, MA

The original buildings are of masonry and brick construction. New construction consists of a poured-in-place basement/first level parking garage, with a wood frame, brick veneer structure for upper floor housing units above. The building is designed with heat pumps and perimeter radiators, providing central heating and air conditioning.

The project was designed to meet all state energy codes and guidelines.

The giant industrial chimney was restored, and a new water main loop through the site was added, benefiting the adjacent town as well as the complex.

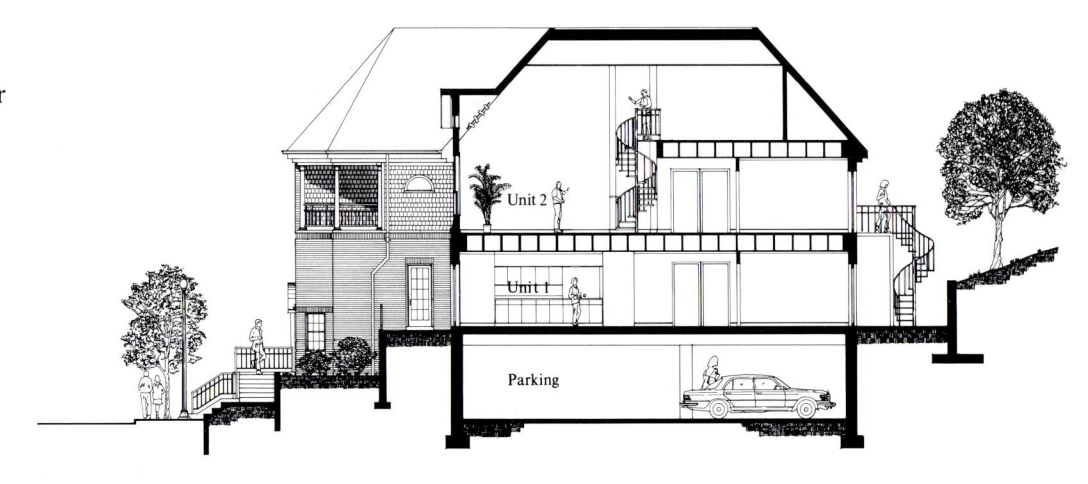

SECOND LEVEL

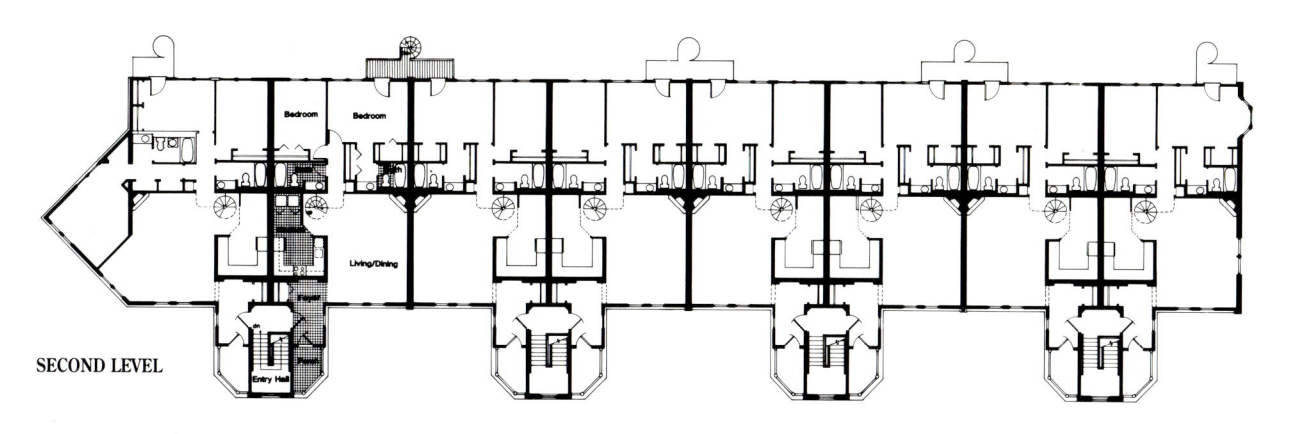

Photography: Nick Wheeler

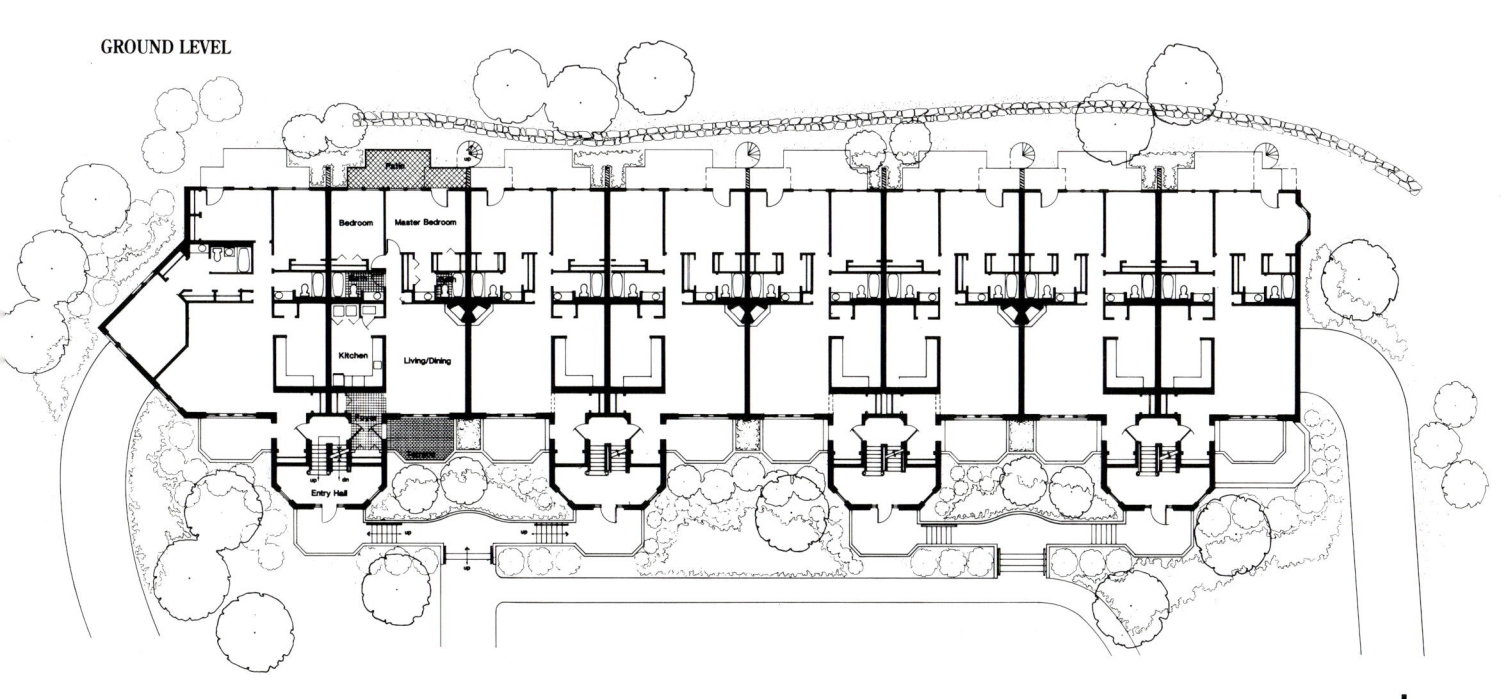

GROUND LEVEL

77

Excellence

The Clay Street Condominiums on Nob Hill are a reinterpretation of San Francisco residential architecture. The flowing lines, graceful curves, and undulating interiors are a nod to the exuberant architecture of James Francis Dunn, who built a score or more of curvaceous baroque confections around the city in the early 20th century. With sensitivity to organic architectural expression, the Clay Street Condominiums significantly reinterpret a well-known and traditional element of San Francisco architecture, the bay window. The elegance of Nob Hill is emphasized as the building outwardly responds to the powerful physical context of urban San Francisco.

The condominium building occupies the top of a hill. Although the neighborhood is dense with buildings, the crest offers views out to the north of Coit Tower, Russian Hill, and the bay beyond.

contd.

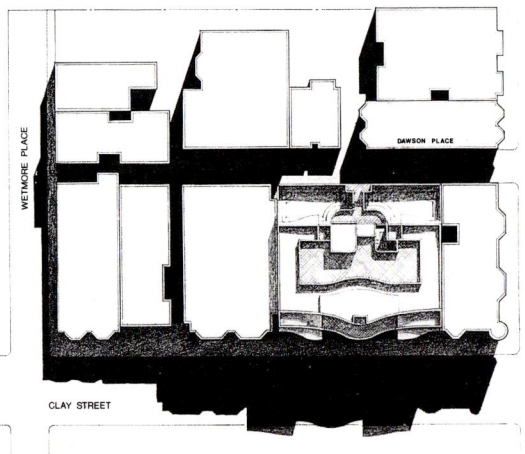

SITE PLAN

Photography: Magnus Stark

CLAY STREET ELEVATION

PROJECT
Clay Street Condominiums
San Francisco, CA

ARCHITECT
Donald MacDonald, FAIA
MacDonald Architects
165 Page Street
San Francisco, CA 94102
Telephone (415) 554 0205

OWNER
Ottman Properties
Munich, Germany

Size and Capacity
Number of units - 11
Gross square feet - 16,900
Ratio of gross: Net - 1.5

Construction Type
New

Construction Cost
$1.8 million

Status
Complete, February 1986

Engineers
Putterman-Davis
San Francisco, CA
Structural Engineer

Edward Brady, P.E.
San Carlos, CA
Mechanical Engineer

Larry Putterman
San Francisco, CA
Civil Engineer

Contractor
Dome Construction
San Francisco, CA

NORTH/SOUTH SECTION

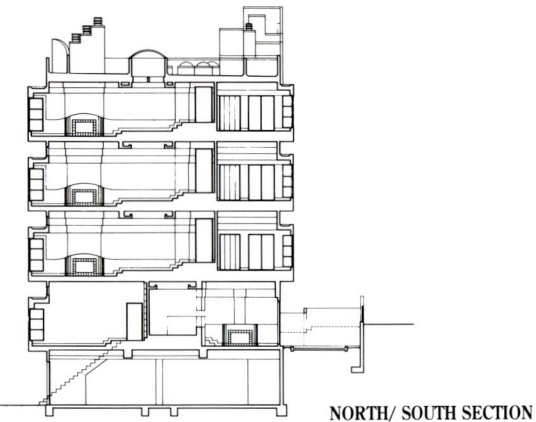

The front facade is akin to the roller coaster terrain of the city and the building's top mirrors the crest of the hill. The exterior colors are similar to those of neighboring buildings. Inside are 11 units: nine one-bedroom units on the second, third, and fourth floors, and two two-bedroom units on the first floor. These first floor units are designed with their living spaces to the rear, overlooking a private garden. The nine units above have their living spaces up front to frame the view to the north. There is also a roof deck for the residents' use and a concrete garage at ground level. Although this building's many curves might suggest masonry construction, the Clay Street Condominiums, at 65 feet tall, is the tallest wood-frame building in San Francisco and one of the last constructed before the city adopted the Uniform Building Code in place of its local code. A special permit was obtained to construct the project.

Photography: Magnus Stark

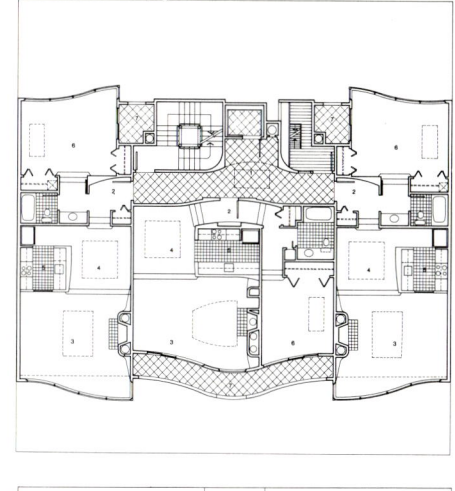

FOURTH LEVEL
1. Hall
2. Entry/Foyer
3. Living
4. Dining
5. Kitchen
6. Bedroom
7. Deck

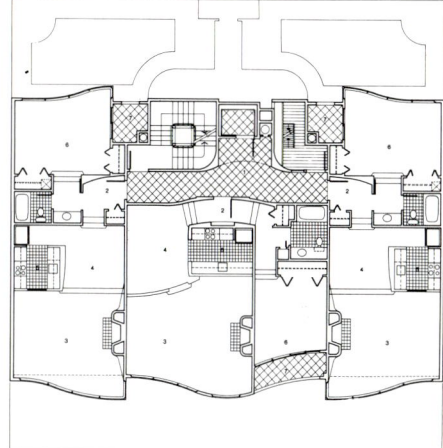

SECOND AND THIRD LEVEL
1. Hall
2. Entry/Foyer
3. Living
4. Dining
5. Kitchen
6. Bedroom
7. Deck

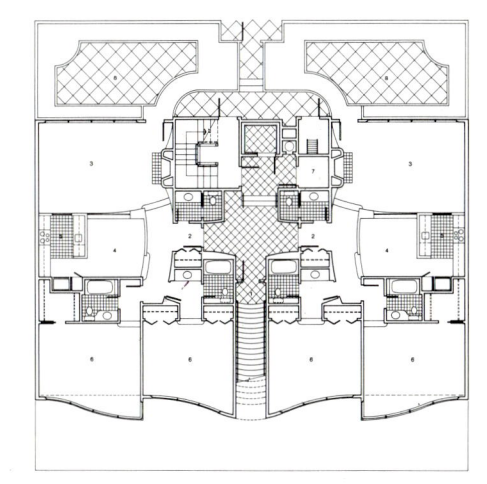

FIRST LEVEL
1. Main Entry/Hall
2. Entry/Foyer
3. Living
4. Dining
5. Kitchen
6. Bedroom
7. Storage Room
8. Patio

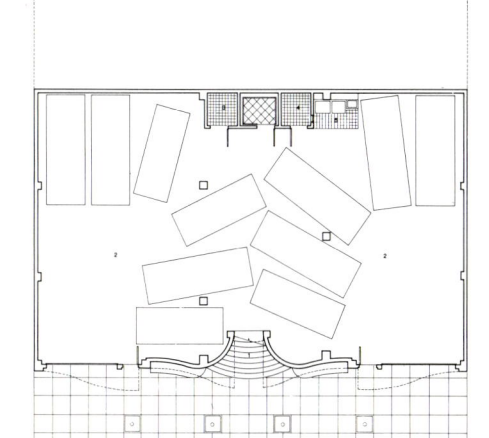

GARAGE LEVEL
1. Entry
2. Garage
3. Mech.
4. Trash
5. Laundry

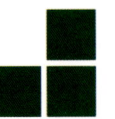

Excellence

The street facades are composed of a varied organization of three different unit facade types providing each unit with either a round bay window, square bay window, or a "stepping forward" porch and balcony. At special locations a corner bay window is employed.

The Back of the Hill Row Houses, 165 units of affordable housing, cover four square blocks and literally create a new neighborhood in a multi-ethnic area of Boston. They are designed to knit together two existing communities previously separated by a "no-man's land" on Mission Hill.

The row houses seek to address major issues of urban housing at four levels.

Broad Urban Design Scale: Responding to both the "second ring" housing patterns of Boston and to the scale of the immediate neighborhood, the row houses celebrate tight urban street patterns and create three new double-sided streets. These generate an urban cohesiveness necessary for this part of the city.

Neighborhood Scale: With strong street forms, the row houses create carefully crafted public space. The garden strips on three streets generate a community focus similar to that found in successful blocks in the nearby South End neighborhood. In addition to being deliberately two-sided, each street is distinguished by a different combination of bay front types and brick colors to be immediately readable by the public.

Individual Units: Three bay front types (round, square, open porch) provide special image and identity to each unit while achieving an economy necessary for affordable housing. Every unit has a private rear yard.

contd.

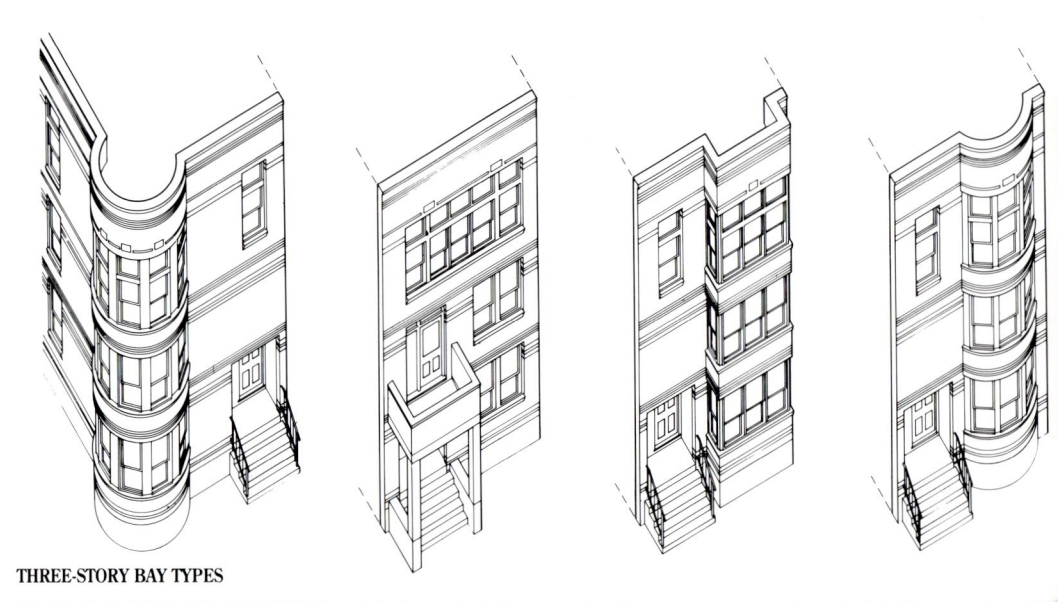

THREE-STORY BAY TYPES

Photography: Steve Rosenthal and Nick Wheeler

B TYPE UNIT ELEVATION

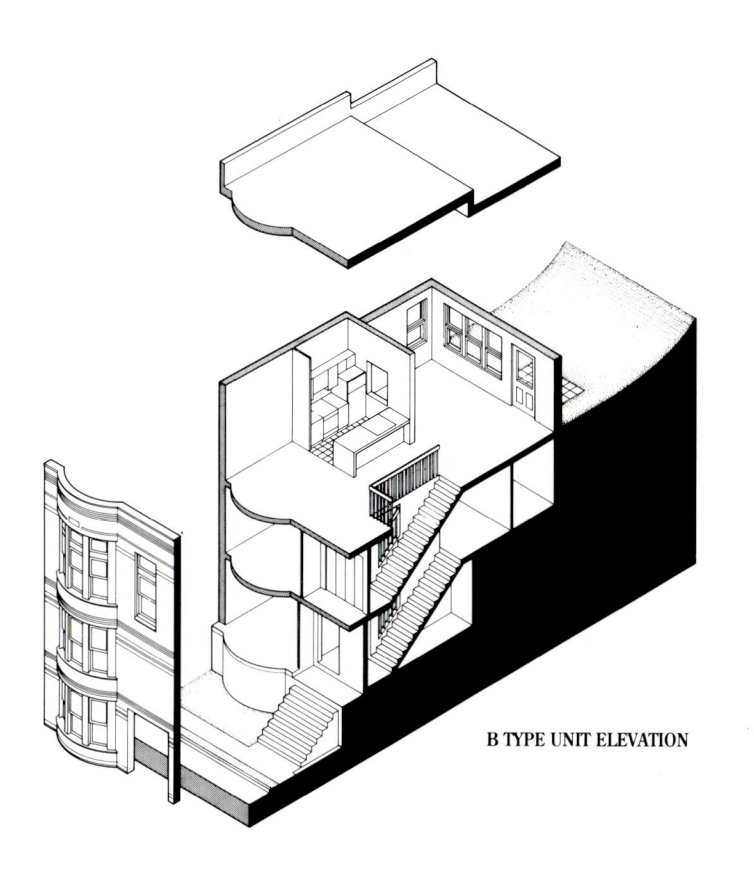

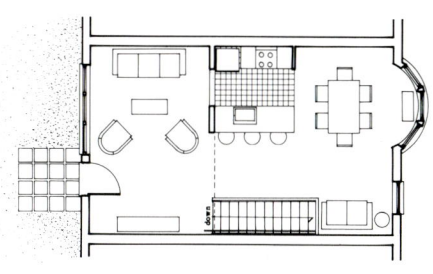

THIRD LEVEL

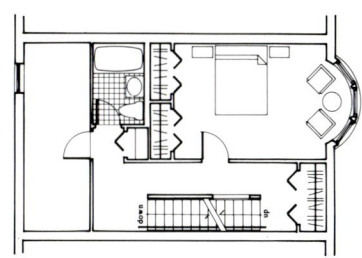

SECOND LEVEL

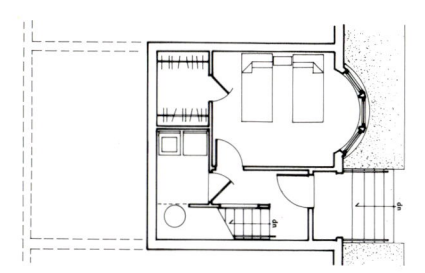

FIRST LEVEL

PROJECT
Back of the Hill Row Houses
Mission Hill
Boston, MA

ARCHITECT
William Rawn Associates, Architects
101 Tremont Street
Boston, MA 02108
Telephone (617) 423 3470

OWNER
Bricklayers & Laborers Non-Profit
Housing Company
Boston, MA

Size and Capacity
Number of units - 165
Gross square feet - 188,372
Ratio of gross: Net - 1:1
Density of gross: Net - 15 u/a

Construction Type
New

Construction Cost
$21 million

Status
Complete, December 1988

Engineers
LeMessurier Consultants
Cambridge, MA
Structural Engineer

Crowley Engineering
Middleboro, MA
Mechanical Engineer

C.A.Q. Planning & Engineering
Salem, NH
Civil Engineer

Consultants
Michael Van Valkenburgh Associates
Cambridge, MA
Landscape Architect

McPhail Associates
Cambridge, MA
Geotechnical

Contractor
Turner Construction
Boston, MA

Unit Interiors: The interiors are distinguished by both a formal living room and a large, open kitchen/dining/family room with an 11 foot high ceiling, which opens to the south sun in 70% of the units.

Photography: Steve Rosenthal and Nick Wheeler

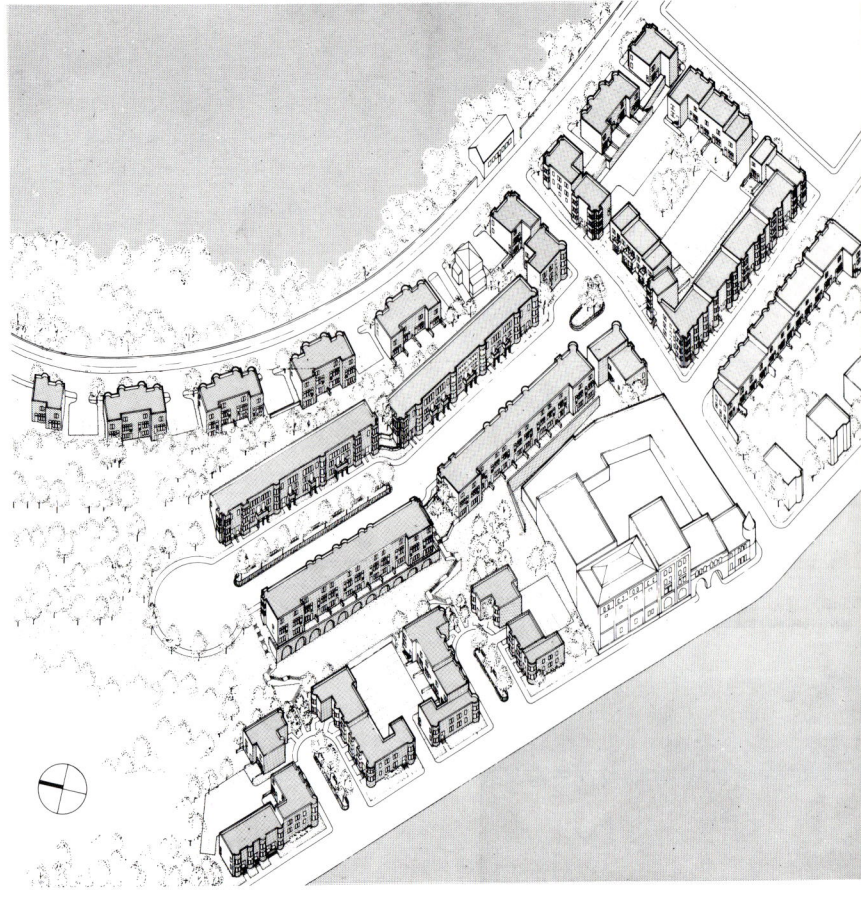

SITE PLAN
The Back of the Hill Row Houses are situated upon an unusually steep site consisting of 11 acres (8 buildable acres with 3 acres designated open space).

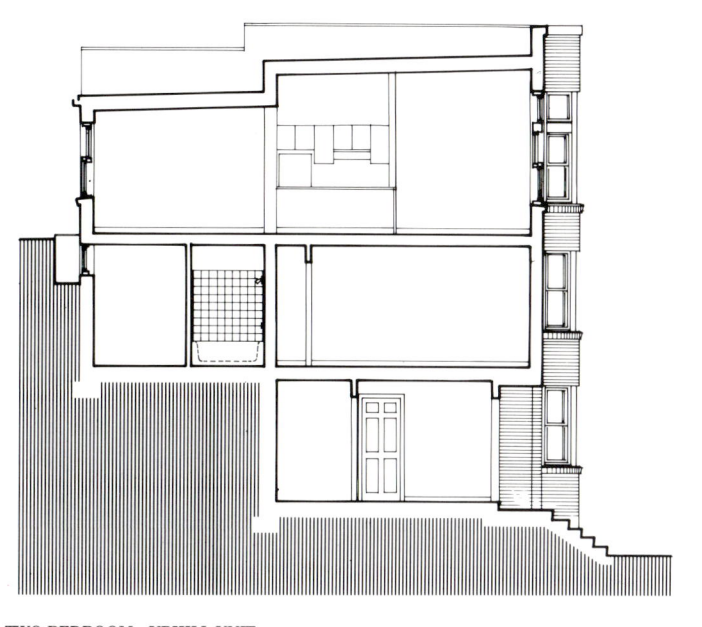

TWO BEDROOM - UPHILL UNIT
All but the one-bedroom units are townhouses in design with direct access to private rear yards from the main living areas. All units are floor through, allowing for maximum natural cross ventilation.

Construction is of multi-colored brick veneer on a basic structure of concrete block bearing walls supporting precast concrete floor planks.

■ *Excellence*

The Charlestown Navy Yard Row Houses (50 affordable housing units for first-time home buyers) are located in an urban village of strong context and historic power on the edge of Boston Harbor. Urban design attitudes generated a housing design responsive to its setting without simply replicating the nineteenth century forms of the Navy Yard. This design, in its responsiveness to context, would deliberately remove the stigma too often attached to affordable housing.

The Navy Yard housing has three major urban design goals:

- The 7-story "front" building maintains and strengthens the sense of First Avenue as the main street of the Navy Yard
- The stacked town houses fit the existing typological pattern of linear buildings running perpendicular to the water in the Navy Yard
- The rounded "tower" piece resolves the street and boardwalk alignments, creates clearly identified public space, and celebrates its water's edge location.

Every pair of stacked row houses is organized with two exposures, each with a water view; the lower unit has a private yard and the upper unit has its own 150 square foot outdoor deck. All but three of the 50 units have water views. Many units include a special kitchen/family room space with 10' 8" high ceilings.

The three parts of the building are connected by special masonry elements, including the brick water table (with its shadow-creating saw-tooth detailing) and a granite checkerboard pattern, which acts as a belt tying together its constituent pieces.

contd.

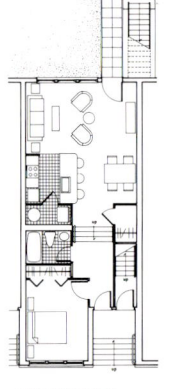

FIRST LEVEL    SECOND LEVEL 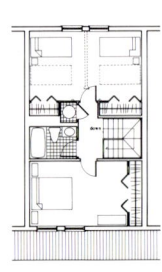   THIRD LEVEL

SECOND LEVEL

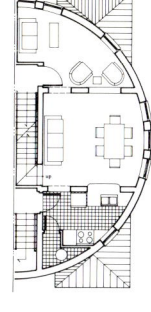

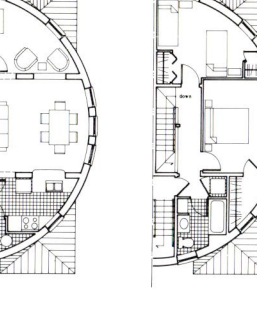

FOURTH LEVEL
Partial

FIFTH LEVEL
Partial

PROJECT
Charlestown Navy Yard Row Houses
Charlestown, MA

ARCHITECT
William Rawn Associates, Architects
101 Tremont Street
Boston, MA 02108
Telephone (617) 423 3470

OWNER
Bricklayers & Laborers Non-Profit
Housing Company
Boston, MA

Size and Capacity
Number of units - 50
Gross square feet - 41,170
Ratio of gross: Net - 1:1
Density of gross: Net - 50 units on a ¾ acre site

Construction Type
New

Construction Cost
$5 million

Status
Complete, October 1988

Engineers
LeMessurier Consultants
Cambridge, MA
Structural Engineer

C.A. Crowley
Middleboro, MA
Mechanical and Electrical Engineer

C.A.Q. Planning & Engineering
Salem, NH
Civil Engineer

Consultants
Michael Van Valkenburgh
Cambridge, MA
Landscape Architect

McPhail Associates
Cambridge, MA
Geotechnical Consultant

Contractor
Mirabassi Associates
Boston, MA

Photography: Steve Rosenthal and Nick Wheeler

87

Construction in precast concrete floor plank on concrete block bearing wall is used throughout for durability, quality, and fire resistance.

Brick arches in Building I, which relate to traditional load-bearing masonry architecture in the Navy Yard, are constructed of solid masonry to avoid the appearance of thin brick veneers.

All the Building II and Building III units are floor through, for maximum cross-ventilation by ocean breezes. Building II duplex units have French balconies opening from their living rooms.

In most units, the living room has been separated from the family room/dining room/kitchen area to distinguish formal and informal living space within the unit.

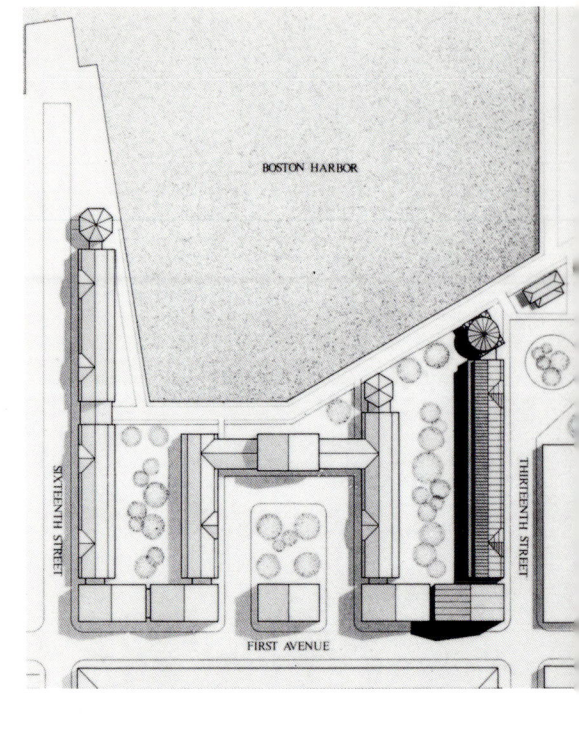

Photography: Steve Rosenthal and Nick Wheeler

THIRD LEVEL

TYPOLOGICAL ANALYSIS

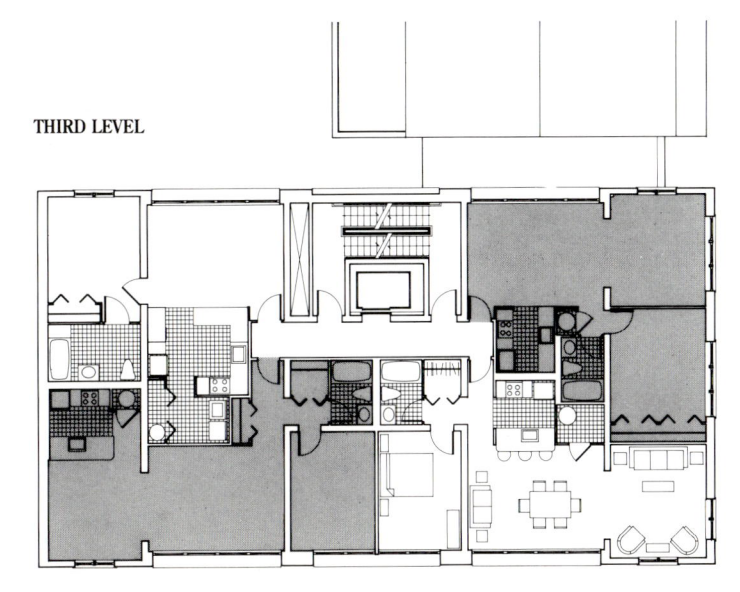

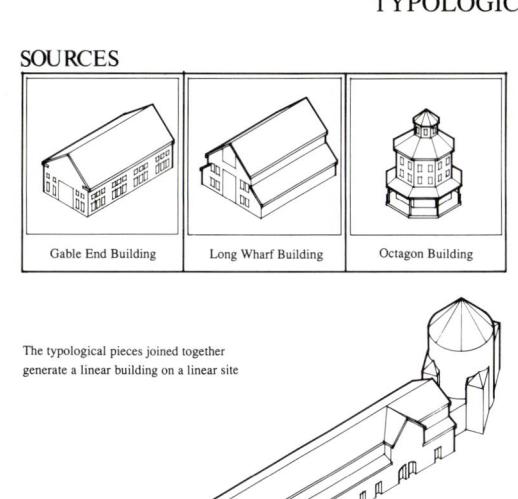

SOURCES

Gable End Building | Long Wharf Building | Octagon Building

The typological pieces joined together generate a linear building on a linear site

The typological pieces articulated by low links preserve the integrity of the parts

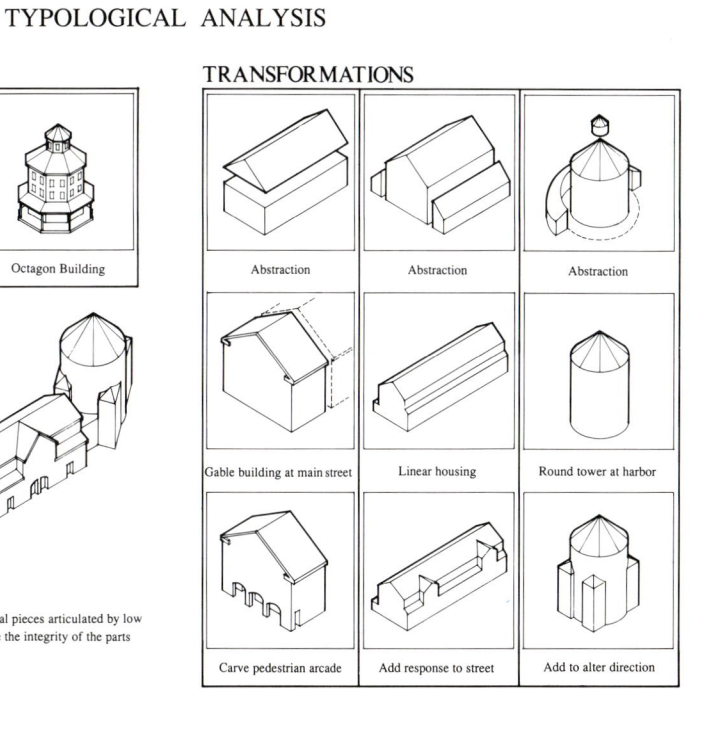

TRANSFORMATIONS

Abstraction | Abstraction | Abstraction

Gable building at main street | Linear housing | Round tower at harbor

Carve pedestrian arcade | Add response to street | Add to alter direction

89

Merit

Photography: Jess Smith

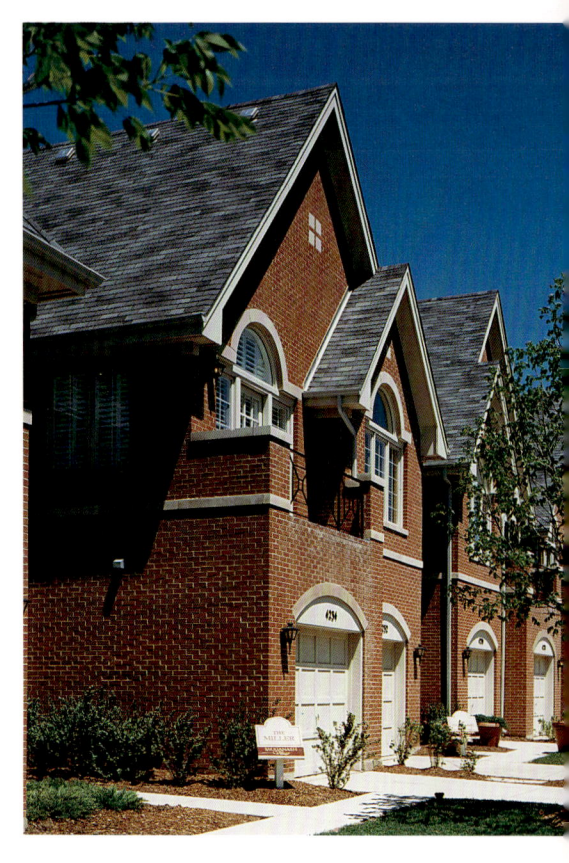

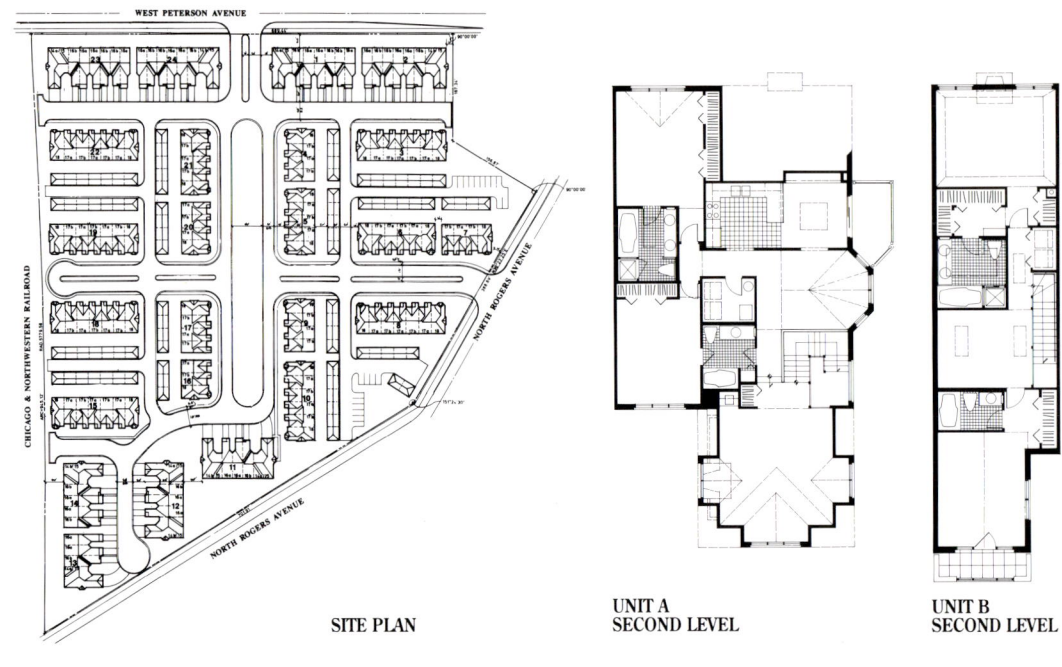

Built on an abandoned factory site amidst a neighborhood of English Tudor, French Norman, and Georgian style homes, Sauganash Village is a town house development that combines the density and architecture of the central city with the open space and landscaping typical of a suburban community.

To preserve the style and character of the neighborhood, the design vocabulary incorporates elements found in area housing. Gables, bay windows, fanlights, and distinctive cut limestone lintels, mullions, and quoins create a unique identity while echoing the past. The red brick facades are reminiscent of the traditional Chicago row house and bungalow. Each building's scale and street orientation recreate an urban architecture friendly and accessible to pedestrians.

The 2-story structures are arrayed around two intersecting boulevards, which create a secluded village atmosphere while respecting the cartesian grid of Chicago streets. A landscaped esplanade is their focus; its fountain, benches, and brick walkway evoking a promenade of the last century.

SITE PLAN

UNIT A
SECOND LEVEL

UNIT B
SECOND LEVEL

STACK FLAT SECTION

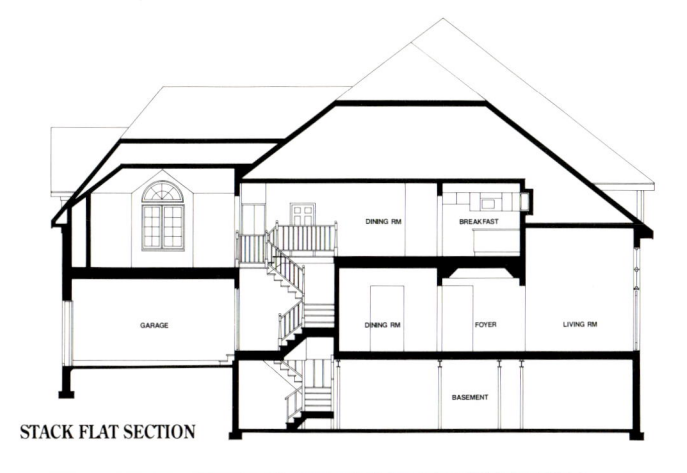

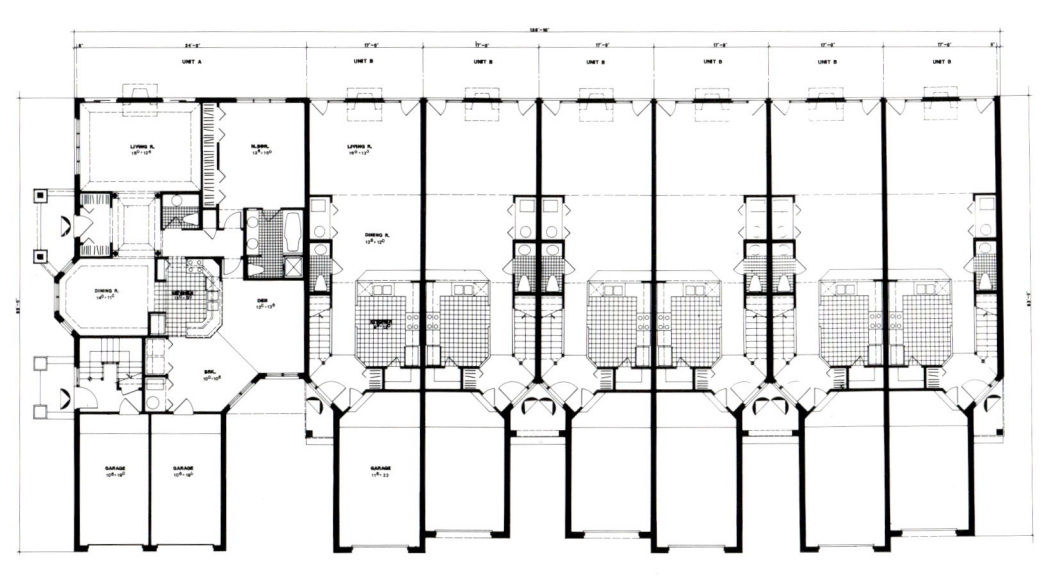

**BUILDING B
FIRST FLOOR PLAN**

PROJECT
Sauganash Village
Chicago, IL

ARCHITECT
The Balsamo/Olson Group, Inc.
One South 376 Summit Avenue
Suite 1F
Oakbrook Terrace, IL 60181
Telephone (708) 629 9800

OWNER
Hoffman Homes, Inc.
Itasca, IL

Project Type
Town houses
Stacked flats

Size and Capacity
Number of units - 144
Gross square feet - 295,284
Ratio of gross: Net - 1.19
Density of gross: Net
- 12.34 u/a

Construction Type
New

Construction Cost
$21.4 million

Status
Under construction
Phase 1: September 1989
Phase 2: July 1990
Phase 3: July 1991

Engineers
Abatangelo-Hason Ltd.
Chicago, IL
Structural Engineer

Chase Associates
Palatine, IL
Mechanical and Electrical Engineer

Kudrna & Associates
Chicago, IL
Civil Engineer

Consultants
Otis Associates, Inc.
Schaumburg, IL
Landscape Architect

The Balsamo/Olson Group, Inc.
Oakbrook Terrace, IL
Land Planner

Contractor
Hoffman Homes, Inc.
Itasca, IL

Merit

This project's uniqueness lies in the way the development team evolved a successful design concept to apply to three different infill parcels. The design consists of 3-bedroom, 2½-bath, back-to-back duplex town houses that present a single family streetscape and reach a density of 10 units per acre.

Two parcels face each other on a brick street in an established neighborhood. The first, approximately one acre, enjoys a corner location. The second parcel consists of two interior lots. The third parcel is a block away and consists of two half-acre interior lots separated by an existing home.

The architects/land planners created a new entrance road for the corner parcel, providing private access to each home. Private access to the interior lot's rear homes was created by a driveway down the middle of each lot. To respond to market demand, a pool was added behind the units in the third parcel.

Because there was no opportunity for rear yards, private outdoor living areas were created on both sides of each home.

Sited in an area of limited affordable land, these homes set the tone for more innovative infill projects that allow buyers to enjoy an older, prestigious neighborhood without giving up the desire for a new home that addresses their current lifestyle.

Photography: Peter Burg

INTERIOR LOT CONCEPT
When two adjacent lots are located in the middle of a city block, a driveway can be brought down between the two lots.

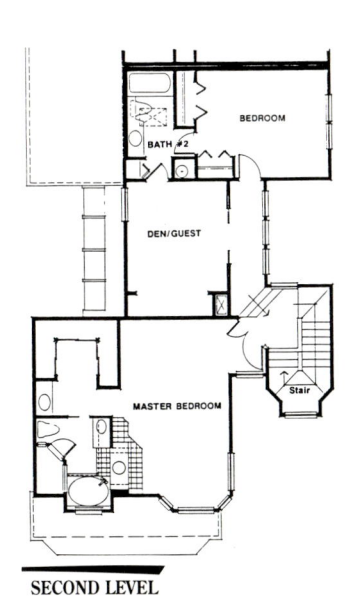

SECOND LEVEL

PROJECT
McIntyre Place
Winter Park, FL

ARCHITECTS/ LAND PLANNERS
Charlan, Brock & Associates, Inc.
2600 Maitland Center Pkwy
Suite 260
Maitland, FL 32751
Telephone (407) 660 8900

OWNER
Renee Stein & Company
Winter Park, FL

Project Type
Back-to-back duplex town houses

Size and Capacity
Number of units - 22
Gross square feet - 44,000
Density of gross: Net - 10 u/a

Construction Type
New

Construction Cost
$3.5 million

Status
Complete, January 1990

Consultant
Charlan, Brock & Associates, Inc.
Maitland, FL
Landscape Architect

Contractor
Renee Stein & Company
Winter Park, FL

93

Merit

Four families commissioned the design of a residential complex consisting of two double-homes on an oceanfront bluff in Malibu.

This project has received two Design Honor Awards from the American Institute of Architects.

The planning issue was to take maximum advantage of the spectacular ocean view without compromising the privacy of each home. Through the use of landscaping, garden walls, and careful arrangement of functional living elements, visual and acoustic privacy is maintained.

The buildings are designed to be energy efficient. The south facing sloped roofs contain flat plate solar collectors for domestic hot water. The north facing clerestory windows provide natural light for the stairwells and master baths.
The operable sash provides for natural ventilation and air circulation.

The buildings are designed to capture light and view. The geometry is pure and the forms are simple. The homes are designed to provide the background for the individual artistic expression and living requirements of each family, but the building envelope is constant so the complex reads as a whole. Individual entry courts and building interior finishes were customized for each home.

The architectural challenge was to provide for and satisfy the individual requirements of each of the four families in an uncompromised multi-family building envelope.

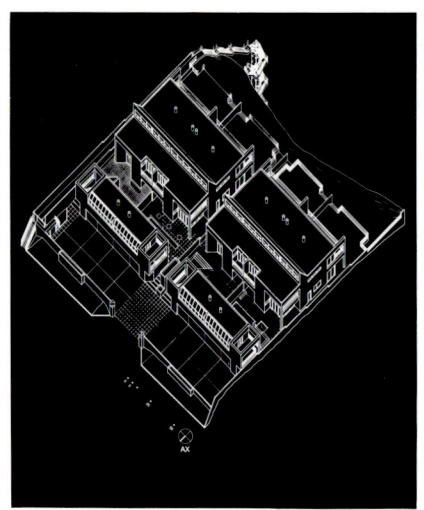

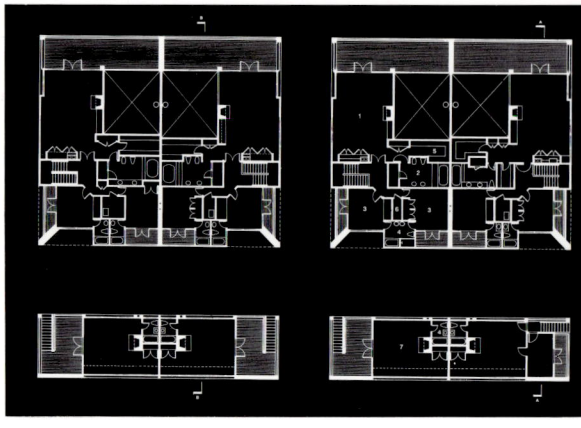

1. Master Bedroom
2. Master Bathroom
3. Bedroom
4. Bathroom
5. Closet
6. Utility
7. Guest Room

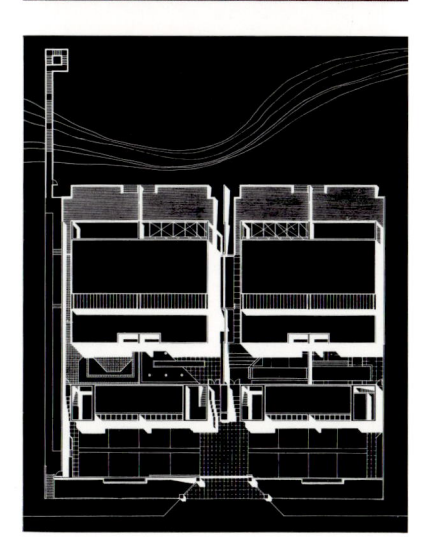

Photography: Glen Allison

PROJECT
Seacliff Homes
Los Angeles, CA

ARCHITECT
Kanner Architects
10924 Le Conte Avenue
Los Angeles, CA 90024
Telephone (310) 208 0028

OWNER
Seacliff Partnership
Los Angeles, CA

Size and Capacity
Number of units - 4
Gross square feet - 20,000

Construction Type
New

Construction Cost
$3.9 million

Status
Complete, August 1987

Engineers
Reiss/Brown/Ekmekji
Sherman Oaks, CA
Structural and Civil Engineer

John Snyder Associates
Burbank, CA
Electrical Engineer

Consultant
Emmett L. Wemple & Dennis Kurutz
Los Angeles, CA
Landscape Architect

Contractor
Winston Chappell
Santa Monica, CA

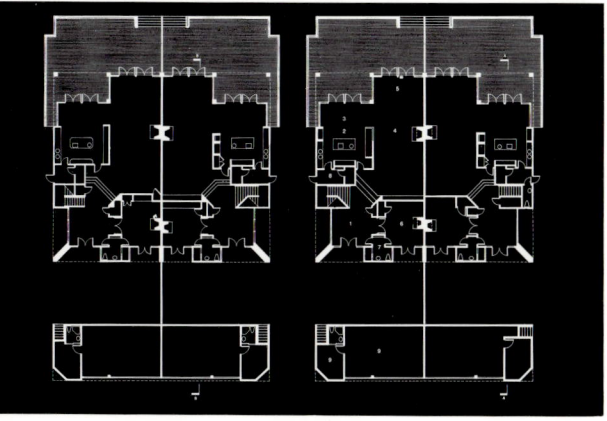

1. Entry
2. Kitchen
3. Dining Room
4. Living Room
5. Tea Room
6. Study
7. Powder Room
8. Laundry/Utility
9. Garage/Storage

95

Merit

Traveling along Connecticut Avenue in Washington, DC, one is met with the quietly arresting presence of the Saratoga. Commanding a panoramic view from atop a hill, the Saratoga occupies one of the few remaining sites for large-scale apartment buildings along Connecticut Avenue. As the premiere street for residential buildings, the avenue provided the paradigm for a more distinguished turn-of-the-century style.

With a keen sensitivity to context, the architect generated the palette for the Saratoga not only from its immediate surroundings, but from Washington apartment house tradition. Housing 187 units, the Saratoga maintains the scale and residential character of a neighborhood. Stately and familiar, with elegant detailing that bears the clean crisp mark of modernism, the Saratoga's decorative appeal comes from the layering of materials and a studied interplay of geometric form. Though a traditional tripartite emphasis is maintained throughout, the horizontal and vertical elements resolve in a remarkably balanced knitting of limestone and brick, leading the eye to explore the whole building.

A strong design sense and responsive awareness to context work together through a clear conceptual framework to answer the needs of both tenants and the neighborhood. With a form that is not only sympathetic to its surroundings but enhances them, the Saratoga makes a welcome contribution to the historic ranks of Connecticut Avenue.

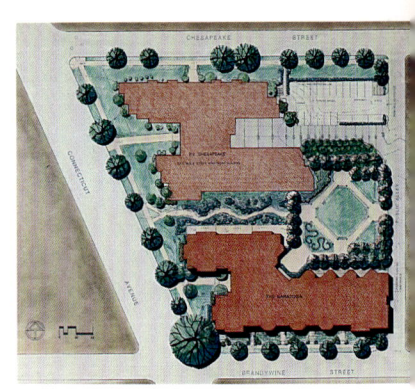

SITE PLAN

Photography: Hedrich-Blessing

PROJECT
The Saratoga
Washington, DC

ARCHITECT
David M. Schwarz/Architectural Services P.C.
1133 Connecticut Avenue, NW
Washington, DC 20036
Telephone (202) 862 0777

OWNER
Horning Brandywine Associates Limited Partnership
Washington, DC

Size and Capacity
Number of units - 187
Gross square feet - 169,000
does not include parking, residential amenities, or doctors' offices
Ratio of gross: Net - 1:.86

Construction Type
New

Construction Cost
$14.9 million

Status
Complete, April 1989

Engineers
Tadjer, Cohen, Edelson Associates
Silver Spring, MD
Structural Engineer

Shefferman & Bigelson Co.
Silver Spring, MD
Mechanical and Electrical Engineer

Consultant
Mortensen, Lewis & Scully Inc.
Vienna, VA
Landscape Architect

Contractor
Double H Housing Corp.
Washington, DC

Merit

A survey of the community undertaken prior to the design of this site showed a need for low-cost senior housing, neighborhood stores, and public beach parking. A mixed-use building was planned with 26,000 square feet of ground floor commercial and retail space, 66 market-rate condominiums, 23 low-cost rental units for seniors, and enough parking to accommodate all the building's functions as well as 79 stalls for public beach access.

While respectful of the community's contemporary architectural development, the design captures the feeling of developer Abbot Kinney's 1911 vision of Venice as a Mediterranean seaside resort community with three to four stories of housing over retail arcades.

To enhance the allusion to the early days of Venice, reproductions of the original turn-of-the-century column capitals, which were the design signature of the town center, crown the arcade that runs the length of the complex.

Despite its high density of 50 units to the acre, an open, airy, Mediterranean feeling was created with the residential component of the project. By designing three triangular buildings connected by open-air walkways, two triangular areas are set aside for open space oriented to the ocean view, one with a pool, the other a lush, grassy area.

A unique aspect of this development is the integration of affordable rental units for seniors with market-rate condominiums. In planning the residential section the decision was made to distribute the seniors evenly throughout the project and give them views of the lively street scene below so they would not feel isolated. Condominiums enjoy ocean views and sea breezes.

Photography: Arden Photography

UNIT B

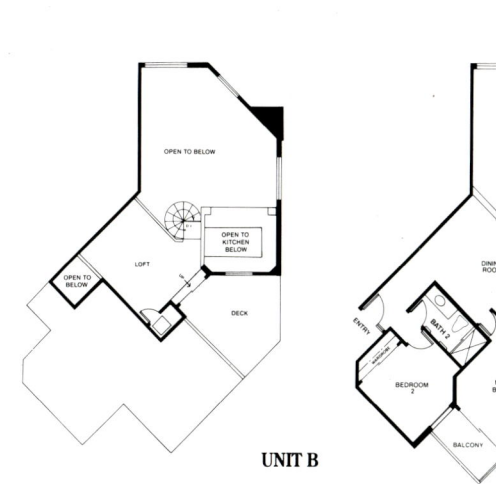

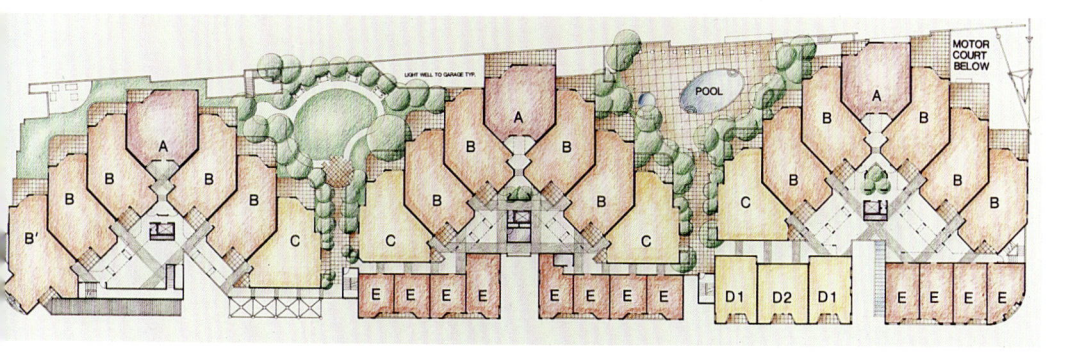

PROJECT
Venice Renaissance
Venice, CA

ARCHITECT
Johannes Van Tilburg & Partners
Penthouse, 225 Arizona Avenue
Santa Monica, CA 90401
Telephone (310) 394 0273

OWNERS
Harlan Lee & Associates
Marina del Rey, CA

The Anden Group
Sherman Oaks, CA

Project Type
Mixed-use building

Size and Capacity
Gross square feet - 132,000
Residential - 102,000 square feet
Commercial - 30,000 square feet
Density of gross: Net - 51.47 u/a

Construction Type
New

Construction Cost
$25 million

Status
Complete, September 1989

Engineers
Jitu Mehta & Associates
Reseda, CA
Structural Engineer

Harold Kushner & Associates
Marina del Rey, CA
Mechanical Engineer

John Snyder & Associates
Burbank, CA
Electrical Engineer

Environmental Technology Inc.
Sherman Oaks, CA
Civil Engineer

Consultants
The L.A. Group, Inc.
Calabasas, CA
Landscape Architect

Lonnie Gans & Associates
Marina del Rey, CA
Art Consultant

Contractor
The Harlan Lee Company
Marina del Rey, CA

99

Cabrillo Village is sandwiched between a river and the railroad tracks and surrounded by lemon groves. Originally a farm workers' camp, the deteriorated board-and-batten cabins were built in the 1930s. In 1975, threatened with eviction and demolition by the growers, the farm workers acquired the camp, rehabilitated the existing cabins, and expanded the village community to include a preschool, a cooperative food market, a chapel, and new farm worker housing.

The design solution is organized around a central green, which steps down the hill and acts as a social space and focal point. All the unit entrances face onto this green, and it leads to the community building, a future baseball diamond, and a view of mountains to the north.

The varying sizes of the families and the different orientation of the units resulted in six different house types, with two-, three-, and four-bedroom units and two elevations. The repetitive nature of the stepped plan allows for a more varied design than the formal rectangular unit plan. The 2-story row houses have front gardens and private rear gardens with two-car carports attached. The kitchen and dining room face onto the private garden. The added facade detailing of the projecting brise-soleil, the off-center windows, and the column and porch all reinforce the focus of the front elevation to the unit entrance.

Aesthethically, the flat roofs and solid walls reference the appearance of Mexican adobe houses. Their massing, sun shades, and earth-related colors suggest traditional architecture, and enhance shadow/shade movement across the facade.

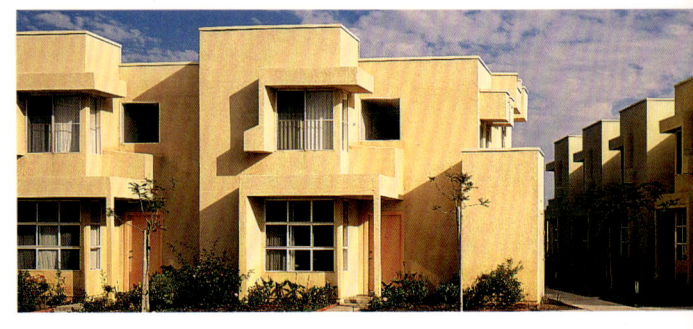

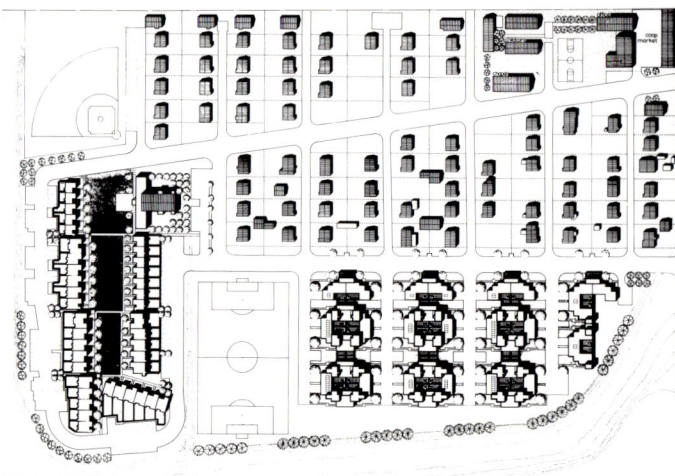

VILLAGE MASTER PLAN

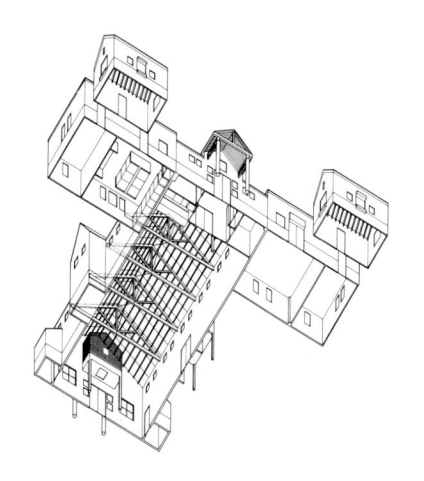

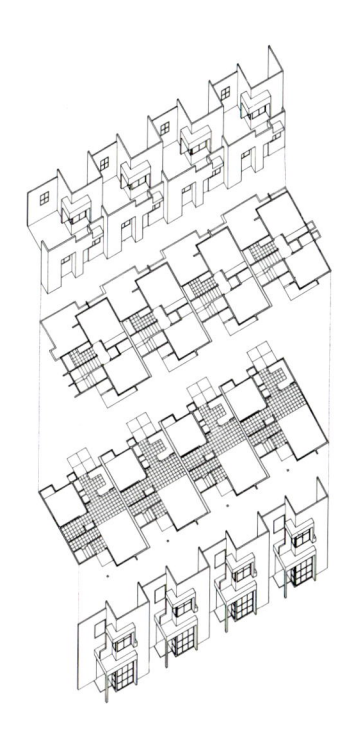

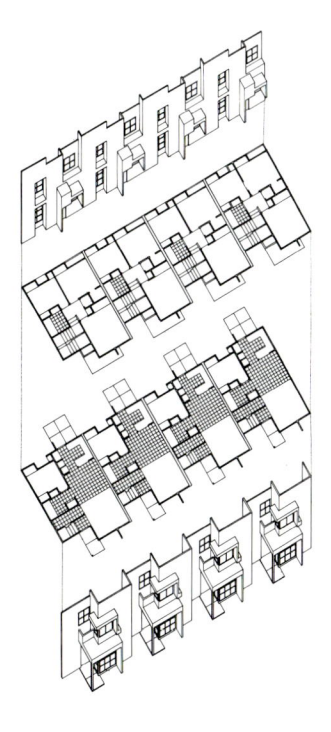

PROJECT
Cabrillo Village
Farm Workers Housing
Saticoy, CA

ARCHITECT
John Vaughan Mutlow, AIA
2536 N. Vermont Avenue
Los Angeles, CA 90027
Telephone (213) 664 4373

OWNER
Cabrillo Economic
Development Corporation
11011 Azahar Street
Saticoy, CA

Size and Capacity
Number of units - 39
Gross square feet - 43,336

Construction Type
New

Construction Cost
$33 per square foot

Status
Complete

Engineers
Ronald L. Rogahn
Irvine, CA
Structural Engineer

Rouhy Dehbibi & Associates
North Hollywood, CA
Mechanical Engineer

Zacharias Vorgias
S. Pasadena, CA
Electrical Engineer

Coory Engineering
Santa Fe Spring, CA
Civil Engineer

Consultant
Barrio Planners Inc.
Los Angeles, CA
Landscape Architect

Photography: Cable Studios, Inc.

Manhattan Place is designed to reinvestigate an old Los Angeles urban form, the courtyard, and to fit contextually into the existing inner city urban fabric of large-scale, older apartment buildings.

The L-shaped project is an urban contextual set piece that edges the street. The 4-story south facade aligns with the brick building to the west, and the east elevation with the stucco building to the north. The ground level community spaces at the apex anchor the corner and externally link the two residential wings, linking the project to the street and increasing sociability for the tenants.

The facades are broken into a series of smaller articulated pieces to reduce the scale, increase identity, and eliminate the monotony of repetition. Each cluster of six units forms a single design element through the projection and articulation of the balconies. This design solution retains the economy of the slab configuration behind. Each balcony cluster is differentiated by variation in the size of the openings and the treatment of the balustrading.

The central courtyard internally links the project's three elements – the south residential wing, the east residential wing, and the communal spaces. The north-south orientation of the east wing courtyard is designed to obtain maximum sun penetration in the winter. The court is partially closed on the north to reinforce the southern orientation. The ice green stucco color along the access balconies blends with existing colors in the community and helps psychologically to make the tenants feel cooler.

A main storm drain crosses the site diagonally, necessitating parking at grade, with all the dwelling units elevated above grade. This arrangement increases the feeling of security for the elderly inhabitants.

The double orientation of the dwelling unit plan provides light, ventilation, and visibility, while the balconies provide shade on the south and east facades.

Photography: Dean Pappas

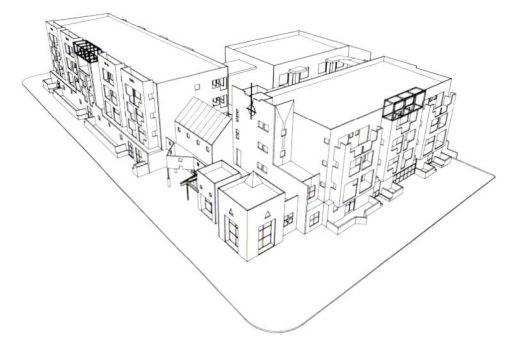

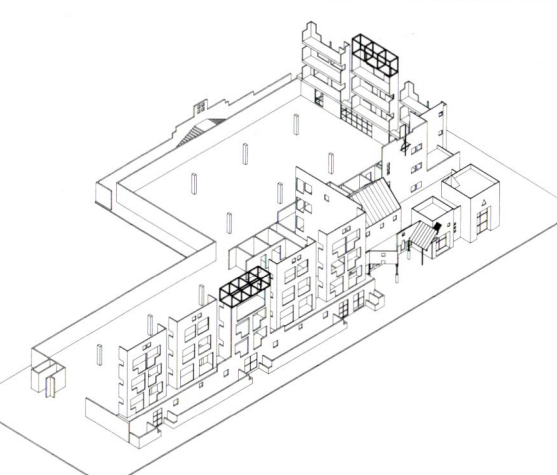

PROJECT
Manhattan Place Senior Housing
Los Angeles, CA

ARCHITECT
John Vaughan Mutlow, AIA
2536 N. Vermont Avenue
Los Angeles, CA 90027
Telephone (213) 664 4373

OWNER
Theodore & Soo Ng
Los Angeles, CA

Size and Capacity
Number of units - 60
Gross square feet - 35,634
Density of gross: Net - 120

Construction Type
New

Construction Cost
$2.75 million

Status
Complete, November 1990

Engineer
Jitu Mehta & Associates
Reseda, CA
Structural Engineer

J.T. Engineering Services
Alhambra, CA
Mechanical Engineer

Zacharias Vorgias
S. Pasadena, CA
Electrical Engineer

Consultant
Barrio Planners Inc.
Los Angeles, CA
Landscape Architect

Contractor
Alpha Construction Company Inc.
Los Angeles, CA

103

Arlington Court, an eighteen-unit town house project, was designed to be a community for its residents while continuing the density and urbanity of the larger city. Built on a one-acre site, this housing enclave is located in Houston Heights, an older, near-downtown Houston suburban neighborhood, platted and developed at the turn of the century.

In response to varying living patterns and domestic arrangements, Arlington Court was planned with four distinctly different unit types, each averaging 1,700 square feet, with two bedrooms and baths, living room with a fireplace, kitchen and dining area, and private outdoor spaces. In accordance with the city's off-street parking requirement of two spaces per dwelling, each unit contains a two-car garage.

The site was arranged so the individual town house faces a garden courtyard, occupying 40% of the site, with vehicular access to the town house garages directly from Arlington Street or the alley. Thus, the front door to Arlington Court is a gate house through which a visitor or resident enters, proceeding through the courtyard to the residences. On axis with the gate house, a 65-foot lap pool terminates the walkway.

It was a clear intent of the design to heighten the sense of space and individual character in what are essentially modest houses. While spatial diversity marks the interior planning, a sense of overall cohesiveness on the exterior results from a uniform material palette of stucco and wood windows and trim as well as the repetition of the prominent stair towers, chimneys, windows, stoops, balconies, and terraces. Still, the variety inherent in the different unit plans is expressed both in the adjoining streets and in the park-like courtyard.

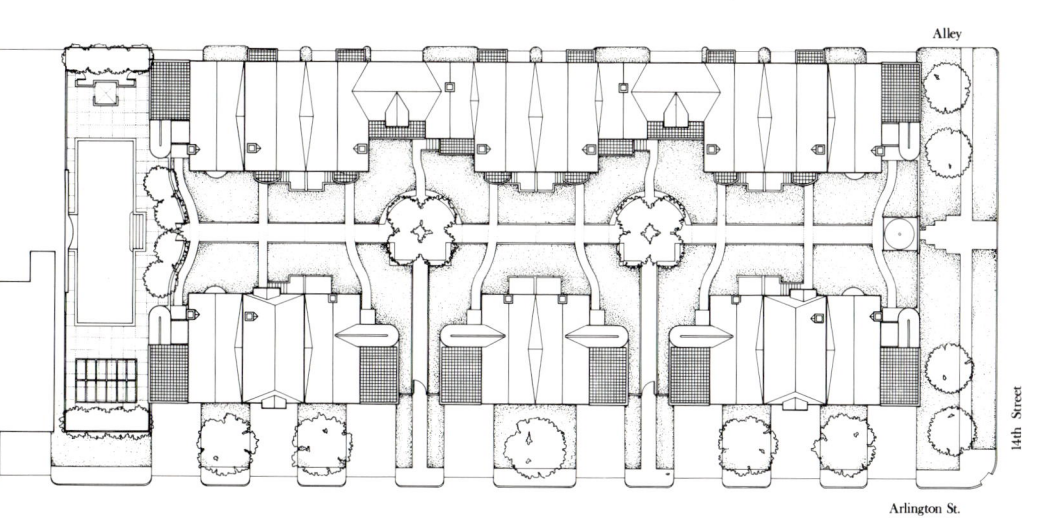

PROJECT
Arlington Court
Houston, TX

ARCHITECTS
William F. Stern & Associates,
Architects
4902 Travis
Houston, TX 77002
Telephone (713) 527 0186

OWNER
Various
Houston, TX

Size and Capacity
Number of units - 18
Gross square feet - 30,600
Density of gross: Net - 18 u/a approx.

Construction Type
New

Construction cost
N/A

Status
Complete, May 1985

Engineers
Cunningham Engineers
Houston, TX
Structural Engineer

Environplan
Houston, TX
Civil Engineer

Consultant
SWA Group
Houston, TX
Planting Consultant

Contractor
Neartown Builders Inc.
Houston, TX

SITE PLAN

105

The J Street Inn, which offers affordable housing for San Diego's working poor, has become the city's flagship example of a public/private cooperative effort to deal with housing the poor.

San Diego's SRO program has become a model for replacing the low-cost housing stock razed by inner-city development. This for-profit project by a private developer was completed with close cooperation and assistance from the Centre City Development Corporation and the city planning department.

The inn is four stories of wood frame construction over a concrete parking garage. It contains a lobby, library, laundry, and exercise room. Each of the 221 rooms has a private bath and a kitchen with a microwave, making the J Street Inn the first example of the city's new "living unit" ordinance.

A central light court, made narrow by the density requirements of the project, is treated as a site-specific sculpture, animated by a grove of fast-growing bamboo and a waterfall to mask noise.

Low cost was achieved through standard production housing detailing and simple, box-like forms. Two architectural events animate these forms, one on Second Avenue at the library and a second, more enthusiastic celebration, at the corner entry. A public deck for each floor offers secure but visible urban activity. Since the inn's opening, the upper deck has been used almost constantly. To further animate the street level, all common rooms are located along Second Avenue.

A high-rise tower of luxury condominiums is under construction across the street, fulfilling San Diego's goal of mixed-use vitality.

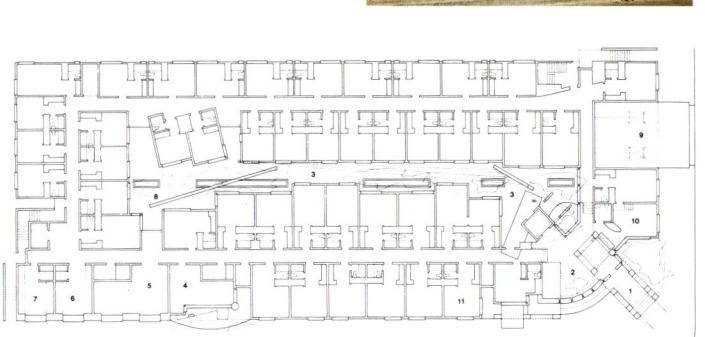

GROUND LEVEL
1. Entry Porch
2. Lobby
3. Courtyard
4. Reading Room
5. Recreation Room
6. Vending
7. Laundry
8. Water Sculpture
9. Garage Entry
10. Office
11. Typical Living Unit

Photography: David Hewitt/Anne Garrison

PROJECT
J Street Inn
San Diego, CA

ARCHITECTS
Rob Wellington Quigley, AIA
434 West Cedar Street
San Diego, CA 92101
Telephone (619) 232 0888

Project Architects
Guillermo Tomaszewski &
Bob Dickens

OWNERS
Chris Mortenson, Bud Fischer
and Shawn Schraeger
San Diego, CA

Project Type
Single-room occupancy hotel

Size and Capacity
Number of units - 221
Gross square feet - 96,451
Density of gross: Net - 387 u/a

Construction Type
New

Construction Cost
N/A

Status
Complete, May 1990

Engineers
AMS Engineering
San Diego, CA
Structural Engineer

GMW Engineering
La Mesa, CA
Mechanical Engineer

Consultants
Andrew Spurlock Martin Poirier
Landscape Architects
San Diego, CA
Landscape Architect

Pacific Structural Concrete
San Diego, CA
Parking Structure Design

Loralee Arnold
Honolulu, HI
Color Consultant

Contractor
Kvaas Construction
San Diego, CA

107

This 37-unit low income development is located in DeQueen, Arkansas, a small rural community with an economy based on farming and lumbering. The development, a mix of one- and two-bedroom units and two-bedroom town houses, incorporates geothermal water-source heating and cooling.

Adjacent residential areas are distinguished by Queen Anne-style Victorian houses and pioneer log cabins. Buildings in the development establish a village-like scale and provide continuity with the historic houses in the area through the use of such elements as high-pitched roofs, beveled-siding exteriors, and historic colors.

A perimeter loop drive allowed preservation of existing trees on the site. A consistent 12-foot planning grid creates a sense of order, while front lawns and a community space are reminiscent of a small-town setting. Small seating areas on pedestrian walkways in key locations encourage social interaction. The planning also allows for small garden plots adjacent to units.

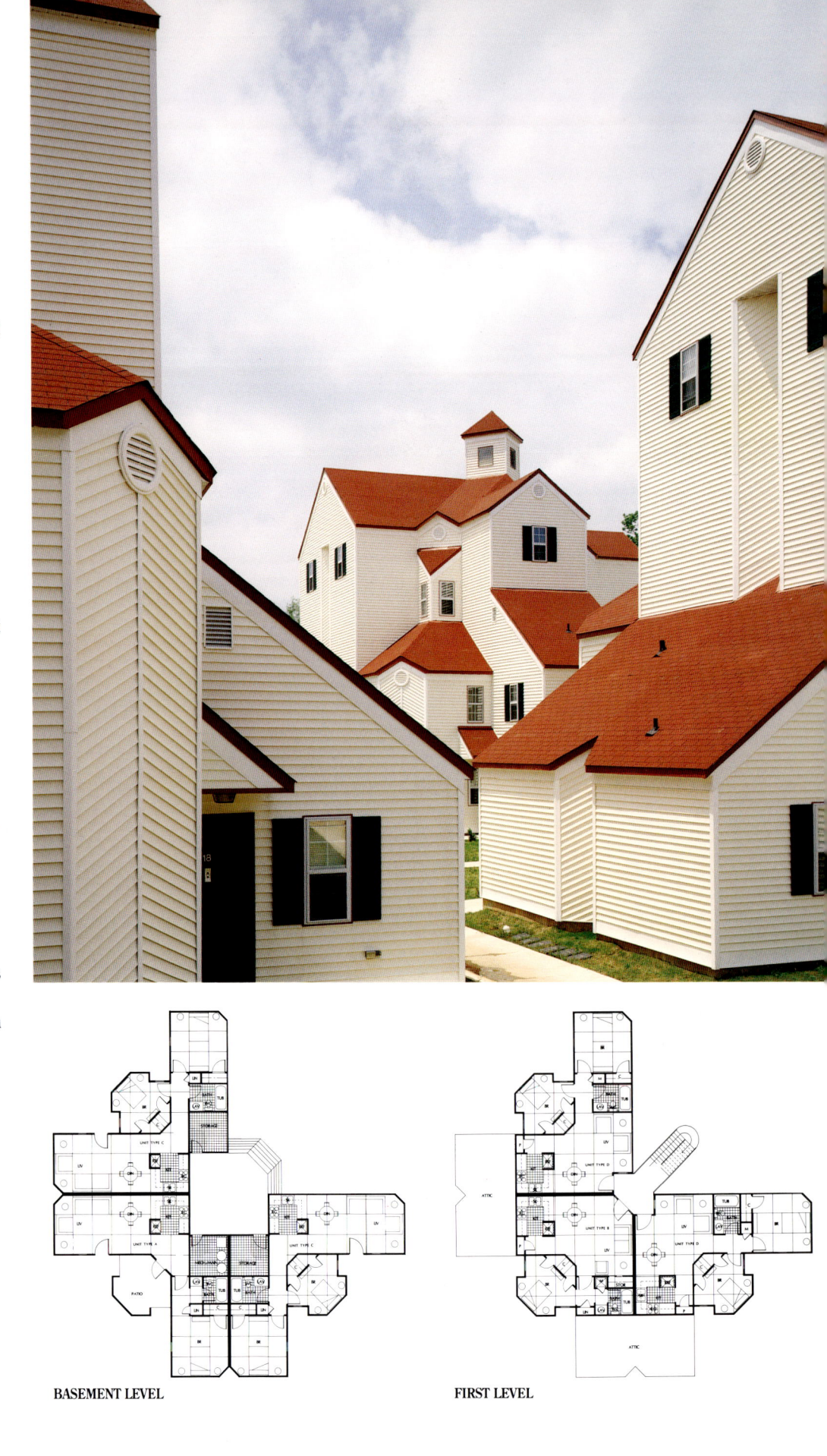

BASEMENT LEVEL **FIRST LEVEL**

SITE PLAN

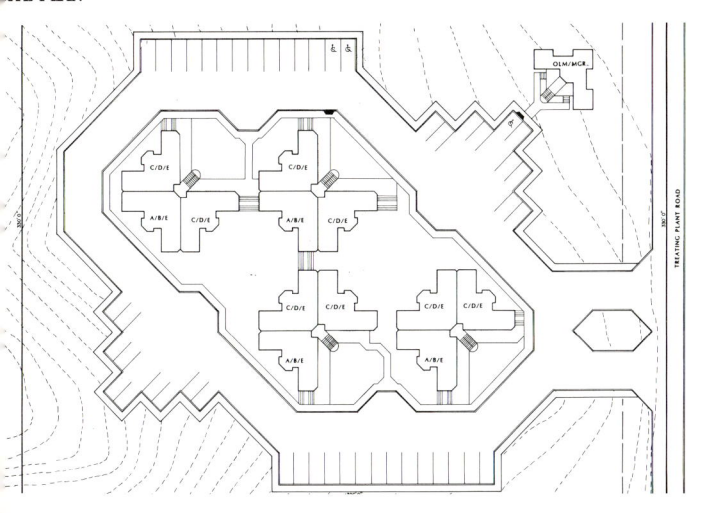

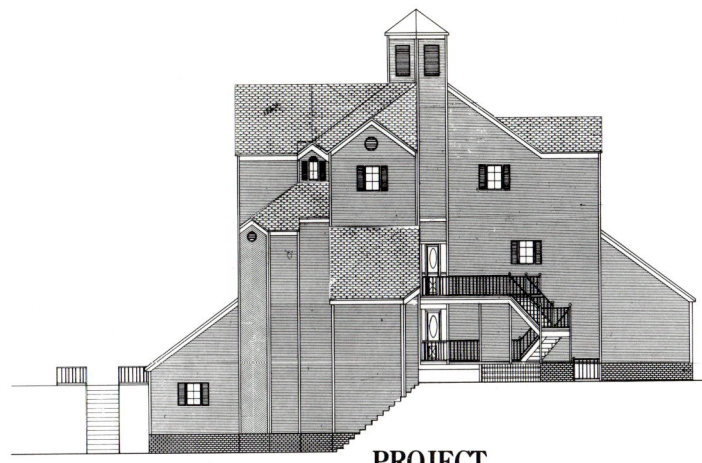

FRONT SIDE ELEVATION

Photography: Timothy Hursley

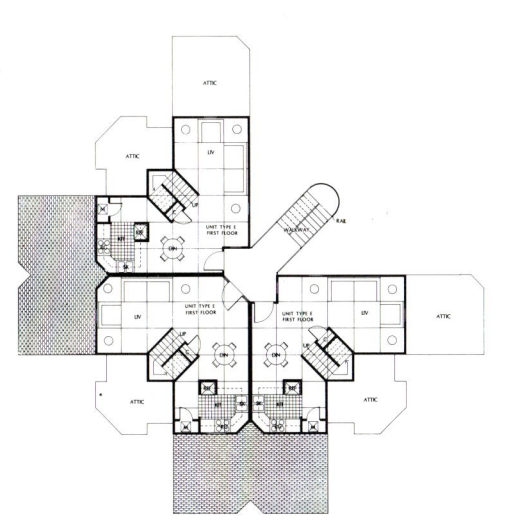

SECOND LEVEL

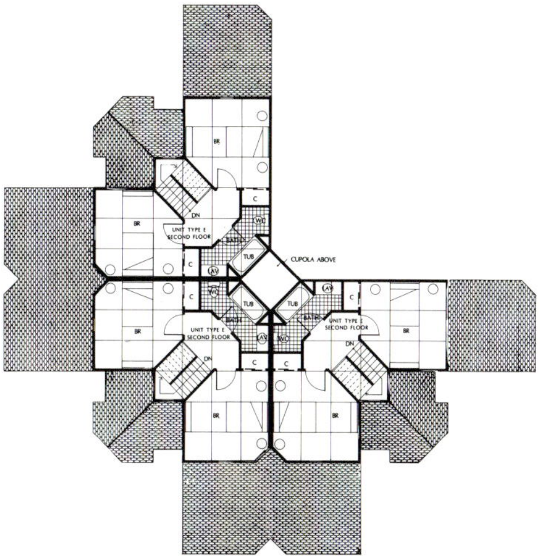

THIRD LEVEL

PROJECT
DeQueen Villas
DeQueen, AR

ARCHITECT
Wenzel & Associates
245 First South Street
Tunica, MS 38676
Telephone (601) 363 1811

OWNER
Tom Marshall
Marshall Planning & Development
Eudora, AR

Project Type
Multi-family

Size and Capacity
Number of units - 37
Gross square feet - 28,166
Ratio of gross: Net - 89%
Density of gross: Net - 12 u/a

Construction Type
New

Construction Cost
$1.1 million

Status
Complete, October 1989

Contractor
Champion Builders, Inc.
Little Rock, AR

109

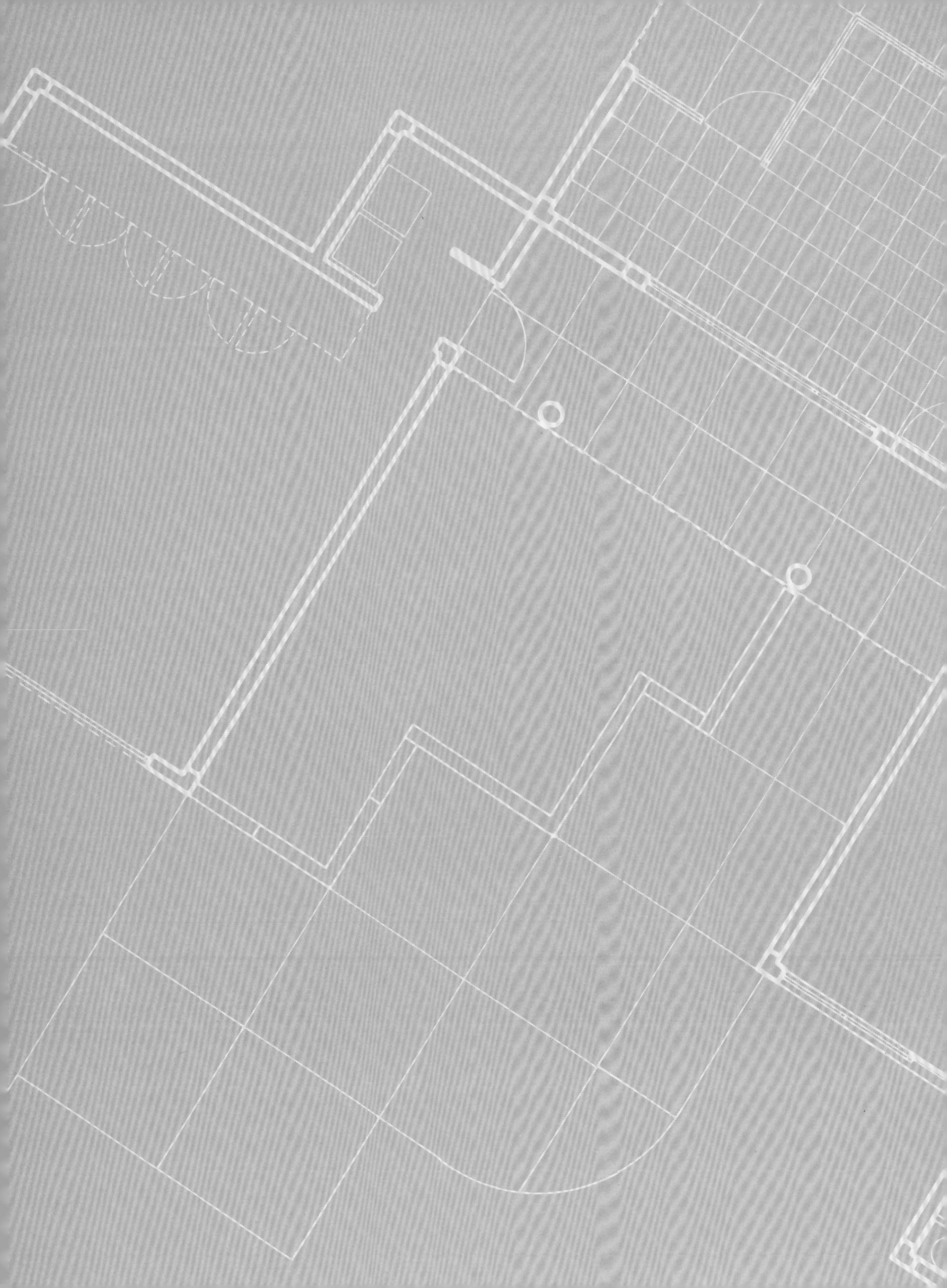

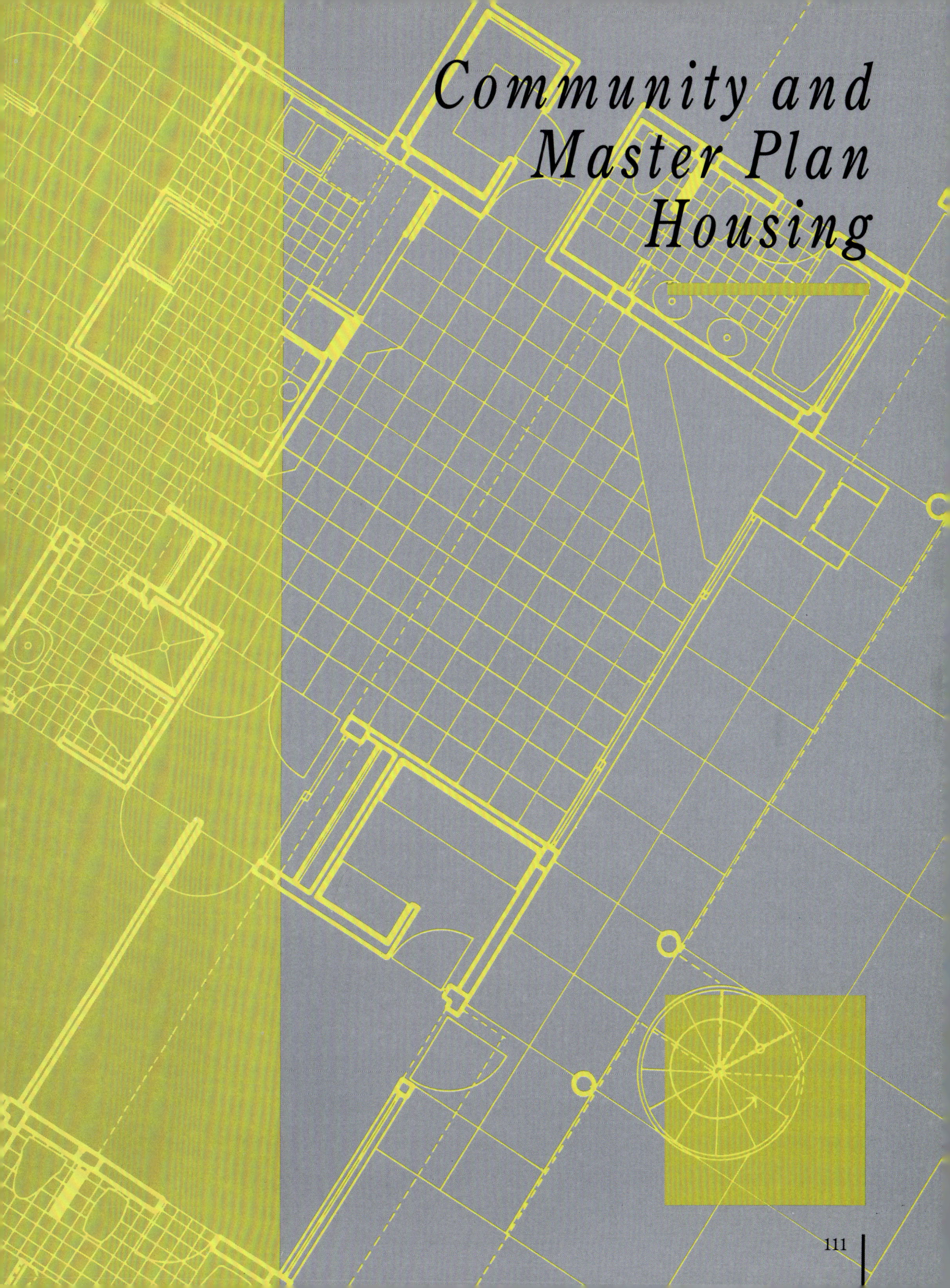

Community and Master Plan Housing

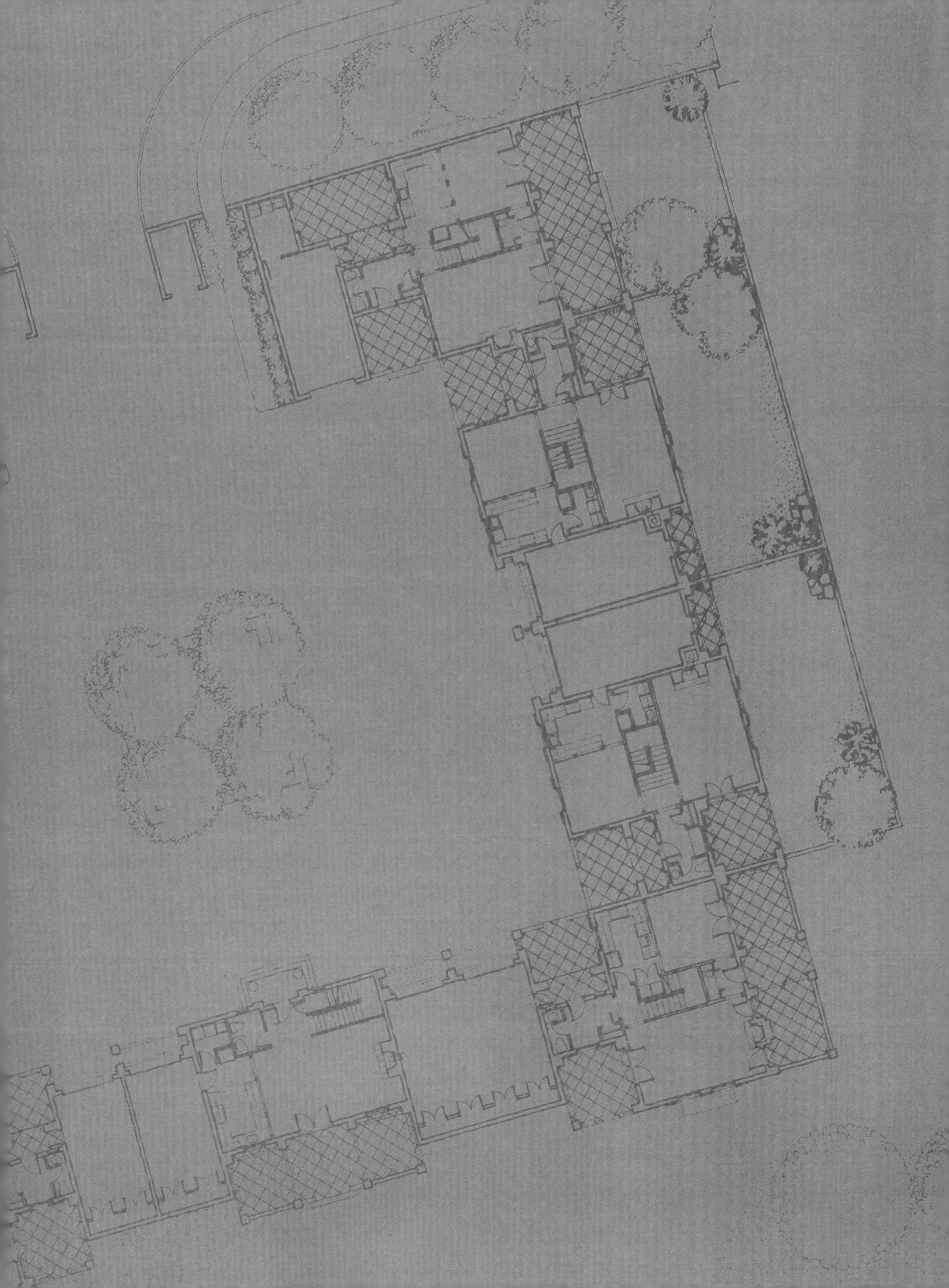

Community and Master Plan Housing

The late 20th century has witnessed a decline in the quality of urban life and a decentralization of urban cores. Low-density bedroom communities have proliferated adjacent to business and commercial centers. Concrete and asphalt ribbons have extended from cities to the outer boundaries defined by commuting convenience. This expansion is the pattern of urban and suburban sprawl. Sprawl has begun a new evolution as centers of commerce have moved to outlying areas, causing an urbanization of suburbia. Fragmented planning, which lacks an overview of the network joining city to city, village to village, neighborhood to neighborhood, has hampered our ability to respond to these changes as they affect both social patterns and the natural environment.

Today the public is increasingly aware of the problems caused by sprawl. A goal of contemporary planning is to preempt sprawl, to accommodate the effects of urban change while preserving and even improving the quality of life. It is now possible to envision the emergence, from unplanned suburbia, of socioeconomically mixed communities whose boundaries are defined in terms of scale and open space, creating separation without wasting land and infrastructure. A planning objective is to create a sense of belonging, to encourage a pride of authorship for inhabitants. Innovative planners are trying to unlock what Sam Hall Kaplan has called the "Holy Grid," to introduce organic edges that create a variety of experiences, as well as focal points and landmarks, to punctuate and link individual elements.

This new vision of community focuses not only on spatial experience but on user needs as redefined by changing social patterns. The suburban community of the future will incorporate living and work spaces together in building groups sited close to community centers that provide support services.

Barry A. Berkus, AIA

Excellence

Built in 1889 on a point overlooking the Rockland breakwater and lighthouse, the Samoset Resort offers the beauty of the Maine coast in a 230-acre, complete resort setting. It was conceived as a place that would provide vacationers with a variety of planned activities from morning until night. Samoset Village, a community of 111 attached housing units built on the resort grounds, was developed to accommodate families and older couples who wanted more privacy than that offered by a hotel but access to everything else the resort has to offer. Samoset Village development was guided by several concepts: (l) To create a place that feels like part of the larger resort complex, yet maintains a separate identity. (2) To create small clusters of units centered around individual open spaces to foster social interaction among residents.
(3) To develop a character of buildings and landscape that is indigenous to coastal Maine.

The village is set within the golf course, visible from the hotel yet isolated by the green expanse of the links. This separation from the large hotel structure allowed the formation of smaller scale, residential building clusters. Within each cluster, 8 to 12 low-roofed, shingled, weathered-gray units surround an oval lawn. All vehicles service the units from the back side of the cluster, where entrance doors to each unit are also located. On the other side of the unit, facing the ocean or golf course view, are the large windows from the living room, dining room, and master bedrooms, as well as the open porches. These porches form a U around the oval, which is edged by plantings of beach plum, bayberry, and roses to separate private porch from community lawn.

contd.

FIRST LEVEL

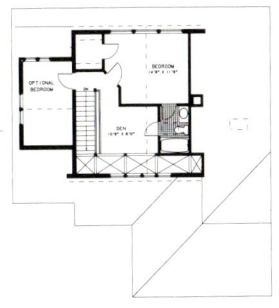

SECOND LEVEL

THE MONHEGAN

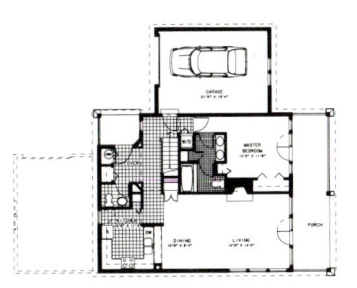

FIRST LEVEL

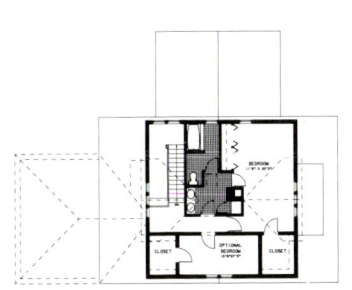

SECOND LEVEL

THE KENNEBEC

PROJECT
Samoset Village
Rockport, ME

ARCHITECT
John R. Orcutt of
Sasaki Associates, Inc.
100 Commercial Street
Portland, ME 04101
Telephone (207) 772 8123

OWNER
Samoset Resort Investors
Rockport, ME

Project Type
Resort

Size and Capacity
Number of units - 111
Gross square feet - 191,724
Ratio of gross: Net - 100%
Density of gross: Net - 2.87 u/a

Construction Type
New

Construction Costs
$4.5 million, phase I only

Status
Under Construction
Completion dates
Phase 1: September 1989
Phase 2: September 1992
Phase 3: September 1993
Phase 4: September 1995

Engineer
Sasaki Associates, Inc.
Civil Engineer

Consultant
Cynthia Plank of
Sasaki Associates Inc.
Portland, ME
Landscape Architect

Contractor
Laukka Construction Inc.
West Rockport, ME

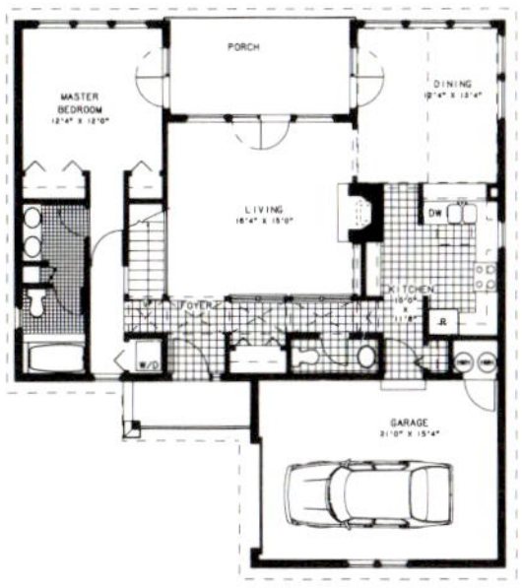

115

The entire cluster is enclosed by white fencing, and grass steps separate the housing from the golf course.

Four unit types comprise the village layout: (1) Sebago (15%), a compact, low-cost unit at the back of the cluster with a combined living/dining area downstairs and bedrooms above. (2) Kennebec (45%), the most versatile unit with a carefully crafted entrance foyer, a downstairs master bedroom suite, and options for up to two additional bedrooms upstairs. This unit makes up the sides of all clusters.
(3) Monhegan (30%), the classic open-air beach cottage with the dining room, living room, and master bedroom all opening onto a gracious porch. The arched window in the upstairs bedroom overlooks the entire oval lawn and ocean beyond. This unit forms the back wall of the cluster. (4) Pemaquid (10%), the largest and most elegant unit, similar to the Monhegan layout, with a majestic stair rising to a bow-front window overlook. Pemaquid is set on the tip of each of the clusters.

Designed to convey a quality of leisure and playfulness, the structures recall the straightforward lines and details of mid-coast Maine summer cottages. Low and horizontal in profile, the homes are clad in wood shingles; broad, overhanging roofs shade large, columned porches. The bungalow style was ideally suited to the need for a generous first-floor plan, including master bedroom, with additional bedrooms tucked under the low roof. The low cottage clusters, softened by a colorful, indigenous landscape, fit comfortably within the golf course resort setting and with respect and appreciation face the rugged beauty of the Maine coast.

Photography: Brian Vanden Brink, Richard Mandelkorn and Sam Sweezy

FIRST LEVEL

THE PEMAQUID

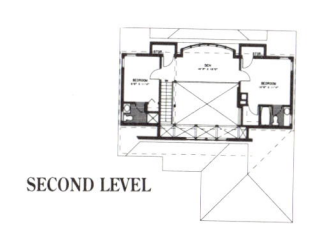

SECOND LEVEL

SECOND LEVEL upgrade

117

Merit

RIVER ELEVATION

This project is the first of 850 dwelling units planned for Harbor Town, a mixed-use residential village on Mud Island in downtown Memphis. It is the first single family house built in downtown Memphis in this century. Therefore, an initial objective of the developers was to identify and establish the appropriate architectural precedent for this previously undeveloped island property in the Mississippi River. The overall goal was to bring the developers' riverfront village concept to fruition and verify that an interior lot could capture the views of an exceptional environment. The major design objective was to take full advantage of the views: the Mississippi River, the Hernando-Desoto Bridge, the Great American Pyramid, and the Memphis skyline. Located on a small corner lot in the interior of the development, the core or service spaces were grouped toward the interior of the property, allowing the major living spaces to experience at least two of the identified views.

Opening the views provides a flowing space while maintaining simple roof forms and overall ease of construction. Exterior materials and details were selected to create a clean impression while recalling characteristics indigenous to the Delta. Specific interior finishes were coordinated not only to give a natural, classical backdrop for the potential owner, but also to accent the views from each space.

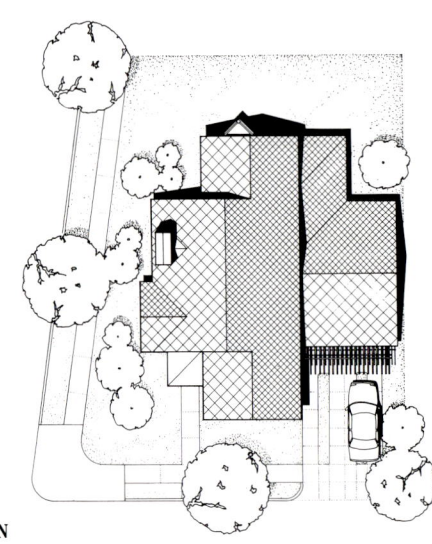

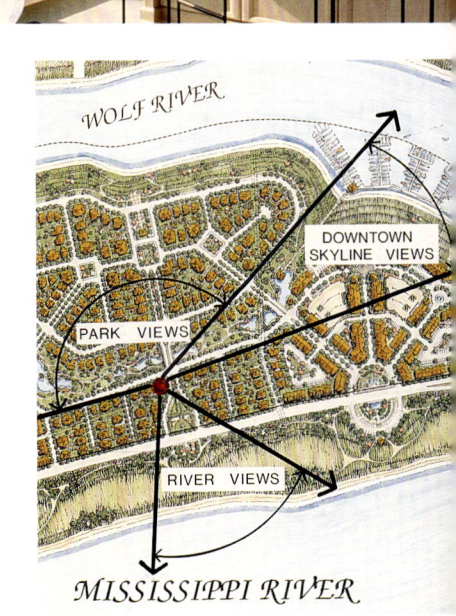

SITE PLAN

WOLF RIVER

DOWNTOWN SKYLINE VIEWS

PARK VIEWS

RIVER VIEWS

MISSISSIPPI RIVER

PARK ELEVATION **FIRST LEVEL** **SECOND LEVEL**

PROJECT
1990 WKNO auction house
Memphis, TN

ARCHITECT
Looney Ricks Kiss Architects, Inc.
88 Union Avenue
Suite 900
Memphis, TN 38103
Telephone (901) 521 1440

Principal in Charge
J. Carson Looney, AIA

Project Architect
Bradford Shapiro, AIA

OWNERS
Island Property Associates;
Henry Turley, Jr., Managing Partner
Memphis, TN

Project type
Single-family

Size and Capacity
Number of units - 1
Gross square feet - 3,145 2,675 heated
Ratio of gross: Net - 1.18:1

Construction Type
New

Construction Cost
$235,000

Status
Complete, March 1990

Engineer
Reaves and Sweeney Engineers, Inc.
Memphis, TN

Consultants
Reaves and Sweeney Engineers, Inc.
Memphis, TN
Landscape Architect

LRK Interiors, Inc.
Memphis, TN
Interior Designer

Contractor
Klazmer/Sklar Homes
Germantown, TN

Photography: Jeffrey Jacobs/Mims Studios

Merit

Located in the remote western mountains of Maine, Sugarloaf/USA is one of the premier ski resorts in the eastern U.S.. The trip from coastal cities passes picturesque farmhouses and paper mill towns until finally reaching the outpost of Kingfield, Maine, an infamous, "end of the trail" town. Fishermen and hunters frequented this part of Maine for years before people began skiing the slopes of nearby Sugarloaf Mountain after World War II.

Recent master planning and development concepts called for turning the ski mountain into a four-season, destination resort. Village on The Green, the first high-quality, year-round housing development to be built at Sugarloaf/USA, sits amid a new 18-hole wilderness championship golf course designed by Robert Trent Jones, Jr.

Village on The Green consists of 94 attached and detached condominium housing units and 46 single-family custom-designed houses. Unlike many golf course developments, housing in this project was not permitted to encroach upon the openness of the golf course. To preserve the wilderness quality of the golf course, housing units are kept inside the site and are not visible from the course.

The architect and the client unanimously agreed that the design of this new development should specifically aim to refer to forms and styles typical of the region. The design of the new dwellings employs elements of the local architecture, creating an important continuity between the region's visual culture and the expanding resort.

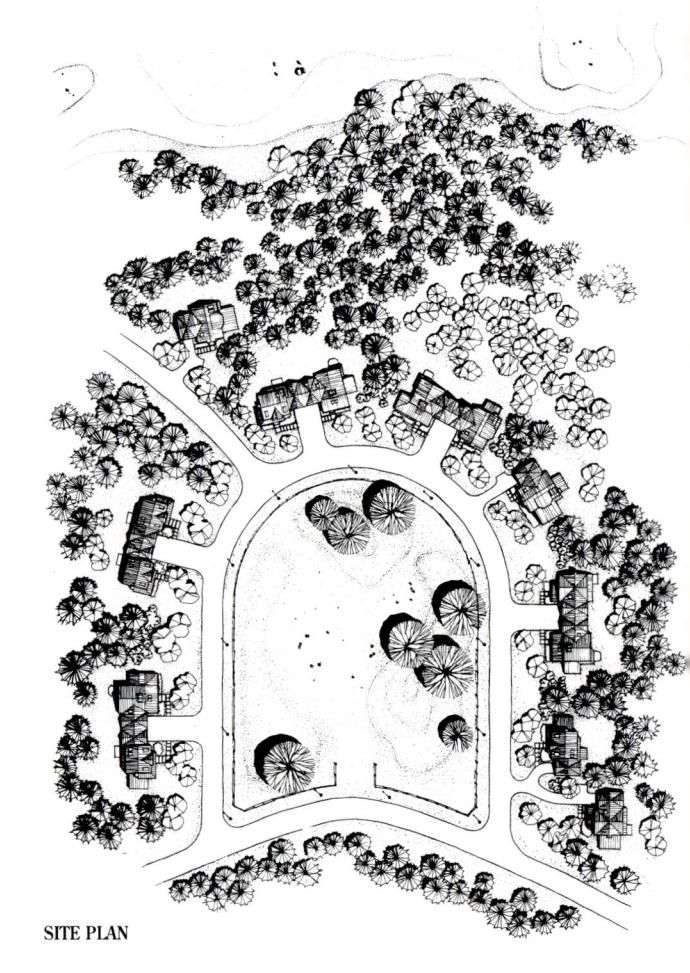

contd.

SITE PLAN

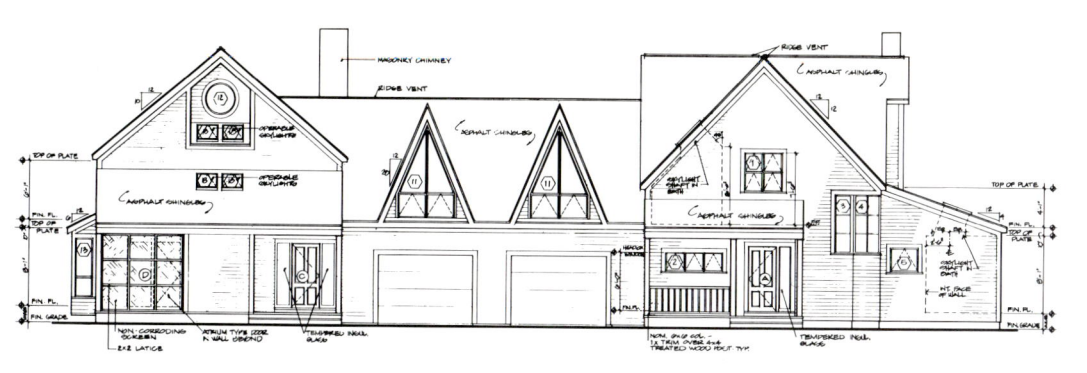

**TYPICAL ATTACHED UNITS
FRONT ELEVATION**

PROJECT
Village on The Green – Sugarloaf/USA
Carrabassett Valley, ME

ARCHITECT
John R. Orcutt of
Sasaki Associates Inc.
100 Commercial Street
Portland, ME 04101
Telephone (207) 772 8123

OWNER
On The Green Associates
Sugarloaf Mountain Corporation
Kingfield, ME

Project Type
Resort

Size and Capacity
Number of units
94 attached, 46 single-family

Gross square feet - 216,388
(attached units only)

Ratio of gross: Net - 100% Net
Density of gross: Net - 1.6 u/a

Construction Type
New

Construction Cost
$5 million, phase 1 only

Status
Under construction
Completion dates
Phase 1: October 1986
Phase 2: future date
Phase 3: future date

Engineer
James W. Sewall Co.
Old Town, ME
Civil Engineer

Consultant
Cynthia Plank of
Sasaki Associates, Inc.
Portland, ME
Landscape Architect

Contractors
Dutch Demshar
Kingfield, ME

Norpine Landscaping
Kingfield, ME
Landscape Contractor

Photography: Nick Wheeler

Acknowledging the simple, late 19th century Gothic farmhouse, a style characteristic of northern New England and influenced by the infusion of French Canadian customs, the condominiums have steeply pitched gables, low porches, simple proportions, and clapboard siding. They are paired to resemble the "house-double dormer shed-barn" arrangement of local dwellings.

Four standard housing units are designed as 2-bedroom base units and are expandable to 4 bedrooms through a series of optional add-on spaces. Optional porches and decks are also available. The location of primary living spaces in each standard housing unit is varied to accommodate optimum orientation for views and privacy.

The focal point of the residential community is a new village green which has been cleared to create an open mountain meadow exposing breathtaking views and providing space for recreational activity.

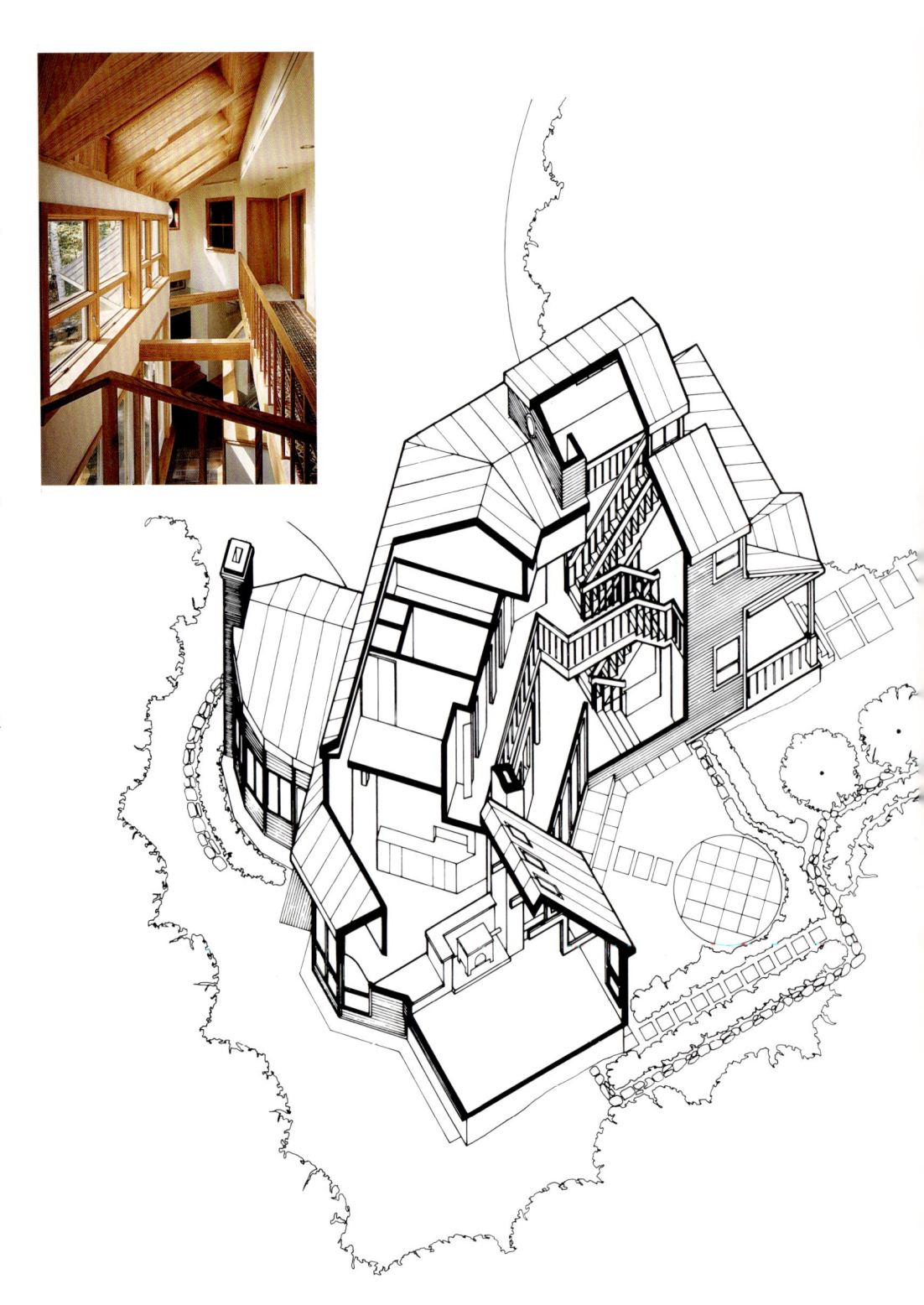

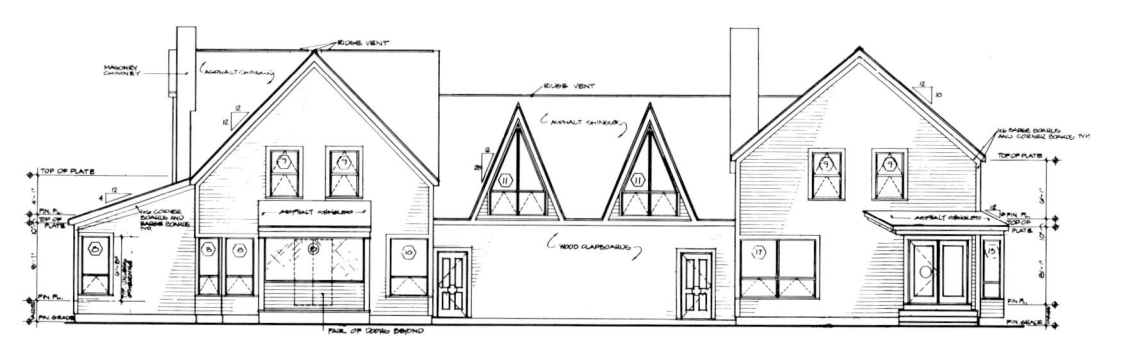

**TYPICAL ATTACHED UNITS
REAR ELEVATION**

photography: Nick Wheeler

123

Located ten miles south of downtown Sacramento, this 800-acre master-planned community is more like a small town than a typical suburban development. Homes, schools, offices, civic sites, shops, and parks are all within easy walking distance. In addition to providing convenient alternatives to the automobile and improving air quality, the project has been designed to make streets and common areas more comfortable and inviting to pedestrians.

Designed with all the ingredients of a classic town, the mixed-use town center is the focus of the community. It offers 150,000 square feet of office space, 90,000 square feet of neighborhood-serving retail, and 1,000 units of higher density housing. Specialty retail shops and anchor tenants will front onto a pedestrian-scale "Main Street." A centrally located village green and town hall will provide a venue for cultural events and community meetings. An adjacent transit stop will be served by feeder buses from the regional transit system.

The working and shopping opportunities in the town center, combined with nearby light industrial and business park uses, will provide job opportunities comparable to the number of residents. The neighborhoods provide a variety of housing opportunities from detached single-family homes, apartments and town houses to in-law studios above alley garages.

Illustrations: Architect

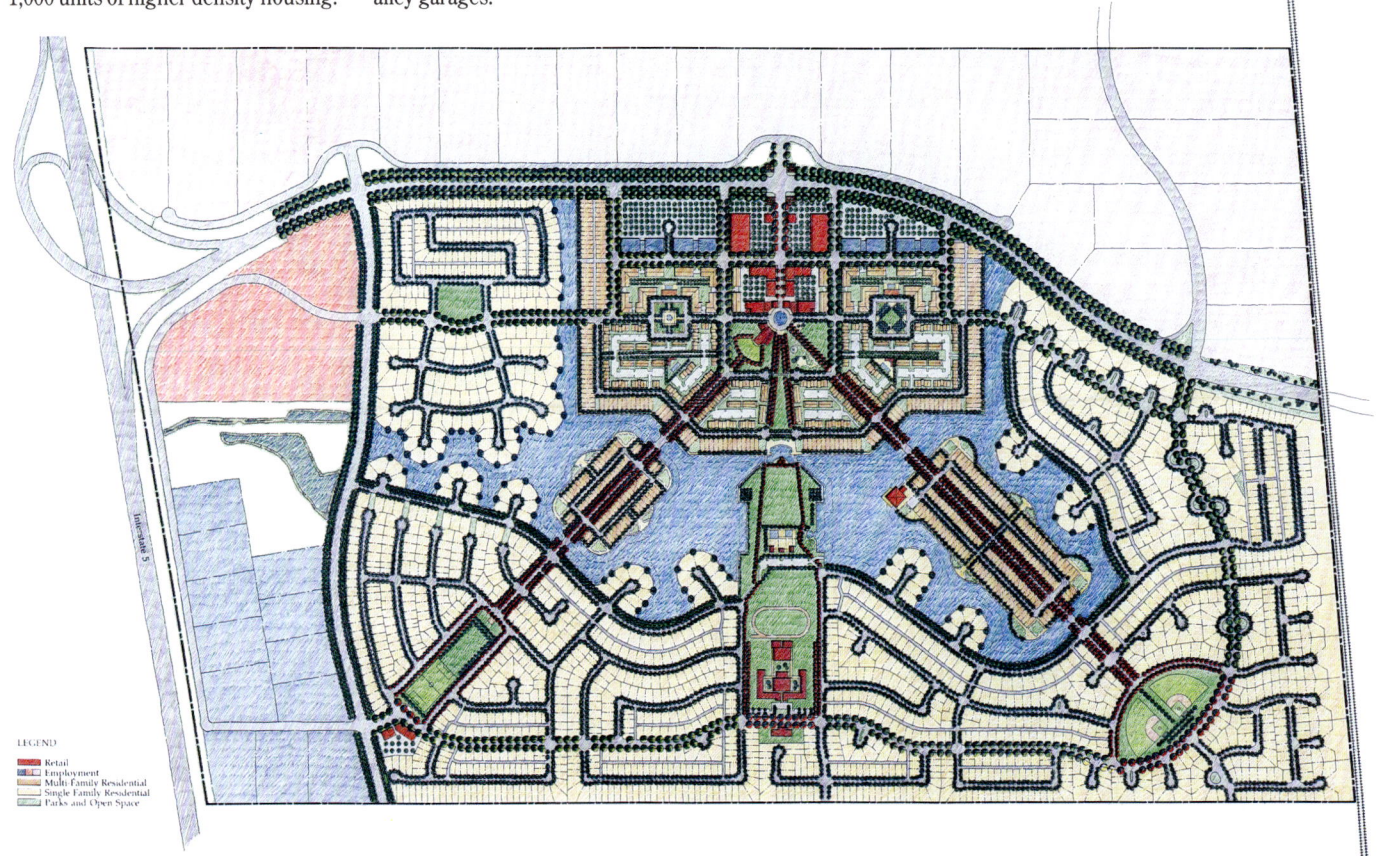

LEGEND
Retail
Employment
Multi-Family Residential
Single Family Residential
Parks and Open Space

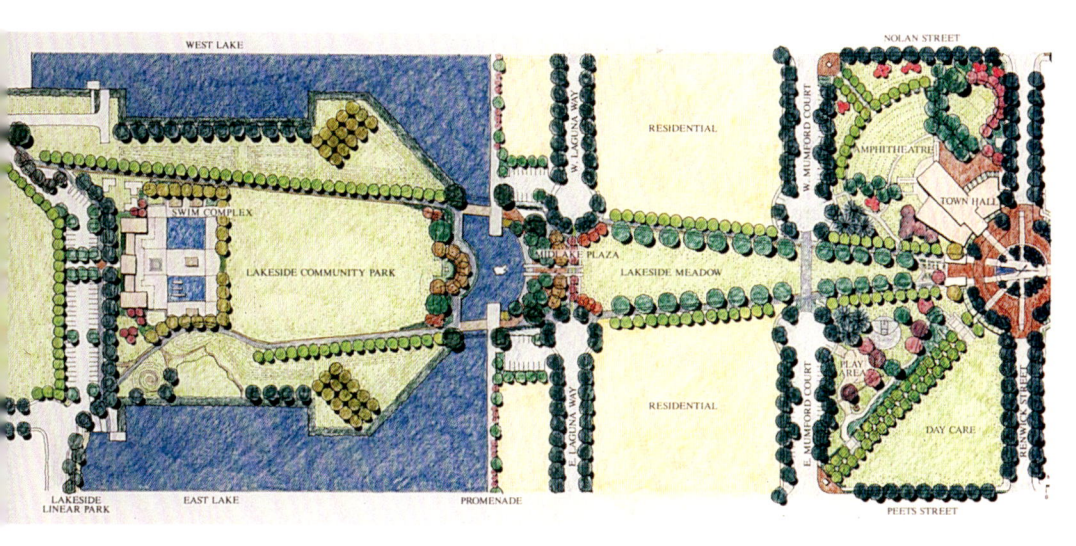

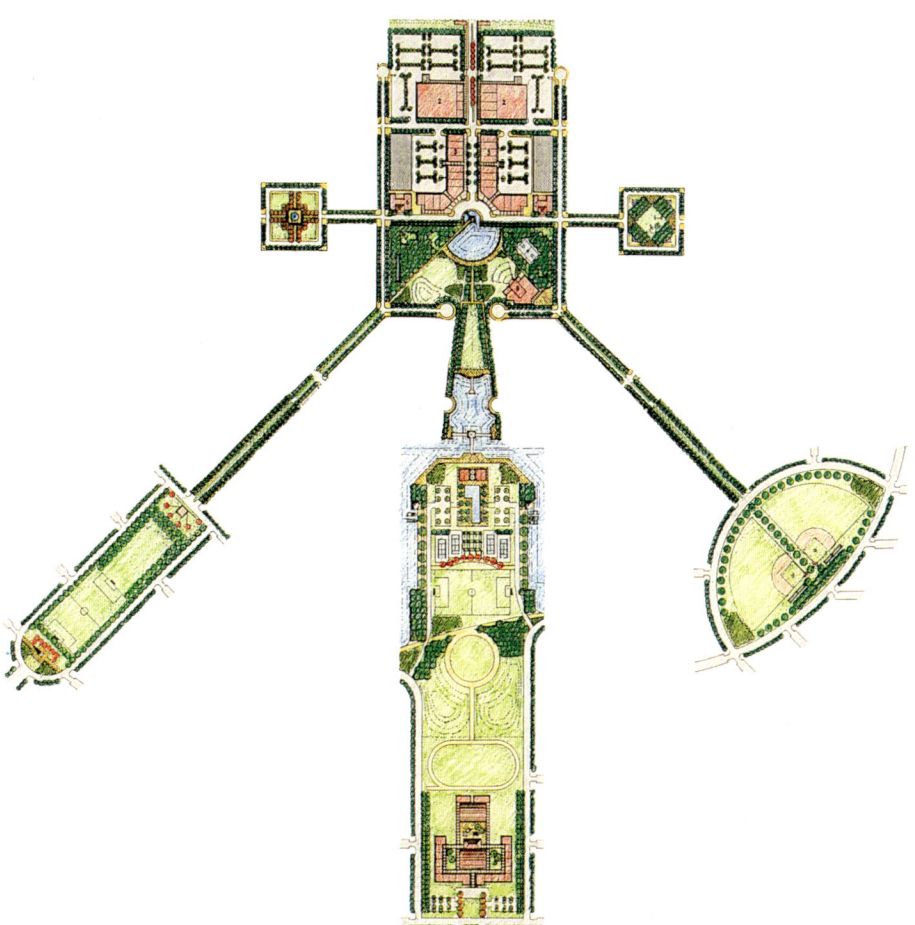

PROJECT
Laguna West
Sacramento County, CA

ARCHITECT
Calthorpe Associates
246 First Street
Suite 400
San Francisco, CA 94105
Telephone: (415) 777 0181

OWNER
Laguna West Partnership
Sacramento, CA

Size and Capacity
Number of units - 3,370
Gross square feet - 800 acres

Construction Type
New

Construction Cost
$520 million (est.)

Status
Under construction
Phase 1: August 1991 (est.)
Phase 2: May 1992 (est.)
Phase 3: May 1993 (est.)
Phase 4: May 1994 (est.)

Engineer
The Spink Corporation
Sacramento, CA
Civil Engineer

Consultant
Ken Kay Associates
San Francisco, CA

125

These houses are part of a new resort community set on the Indian River in Vero Beach, Florida. The houses are an integral part of a community recreation complex that includes a golf club, tennis club, and swim club. The club village is intended to work as a cohesive urban unit with a hierarchy of streets and paths, large urban spaces and intimate courts, community buildings and individually articulated town houses.

Each grouping of houses is composed of four closely related house types interlocked in an orderly fashion that is at the same time relaxed and picturesque. Stucco walls, clay tile roofs, and shutters continue the Mediterranean theme of the downtown, but are here given a more distinctly classical feeling suggesting Bermuda or Barbados.

A private road from the entry plaza leads to the landscaped boulevard that ties together the seven house courts containing a total of 67 town house units. In order to avoid large expanses of pavement, the parking is dispersed along the streets and in well-defined landscaped spaces. The progression from the entry plaza to each individual house is marked by a hierarchy of outdoor spaces that starts from the largest and most public and progresses to semi-private car courts and finally to the smallest and most intimate courts at each individual house.

Photography: Esto Photographics - Peter Aaron

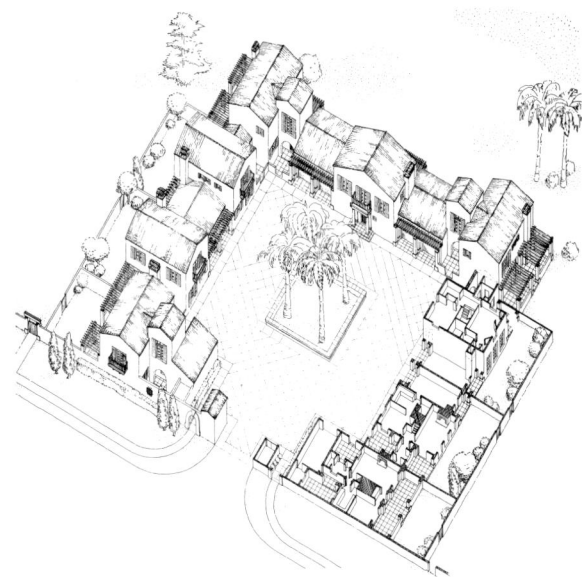

FIRST LEVEL -Parcel P

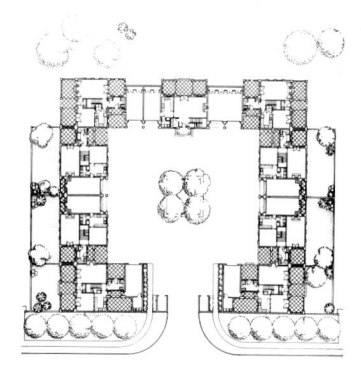

PROJECT
Grand Harbor
Vero Beach, FL

ARCHITECT
Robert A. M. Stern Architects
211 West 61st Street
New York, NY 10023
Telephone (212) 246 1980

OWNER
Schaub Communities
Vero Beach, FL

Size And Capacity
Number of units - 67
Gross square feet - 4,000

Construction Type
New

Construction Cost
N/A

Status
Completed 1988

Engineers
Santiago & Associates
Miami, FL
Structural Engineer

Beindorf & Associates
Vero Beach, FL
Civil Engineer Surveyor

Masteller & Moller Associates
Sebastian, FL
Civil Engineer

Relco Unlimited
Melbourne, FL
Electrical and Mechanical Engineer

Jammal & Associates
West Palm Beach, FL
Soils Engineer

Consultants
Bradshaw, Gill, Fuster & Associates
Lauderdale-by-the-sea, FL
Landscape Architect

Andres Duaney and
Elizabeth Plater-Zyberk
Coconut Grove, FL
Conceptual Land Planner

Clemens Bruns Schaub Architects
Pensacola, FL
Conceptual Land Planner

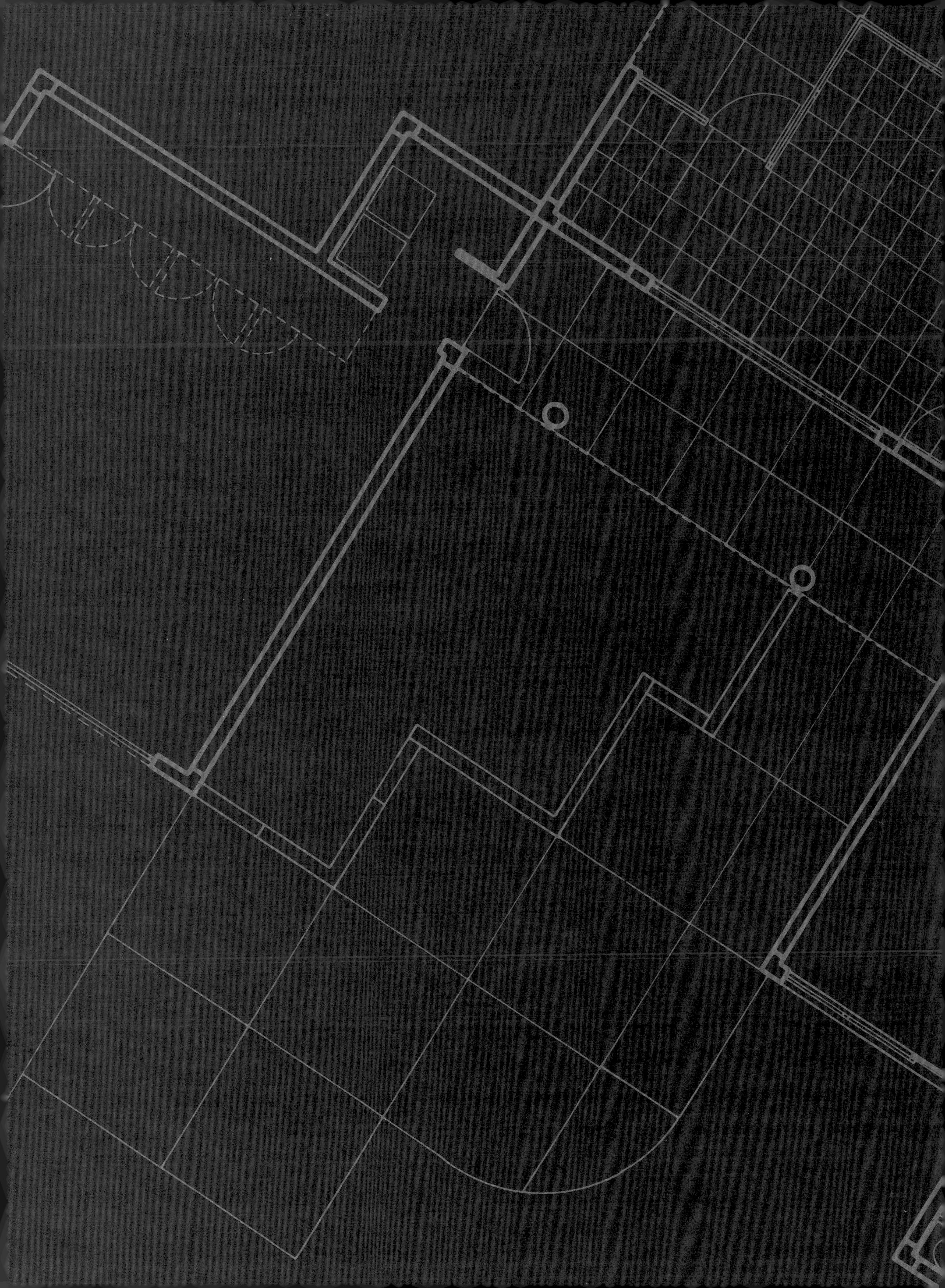

Index

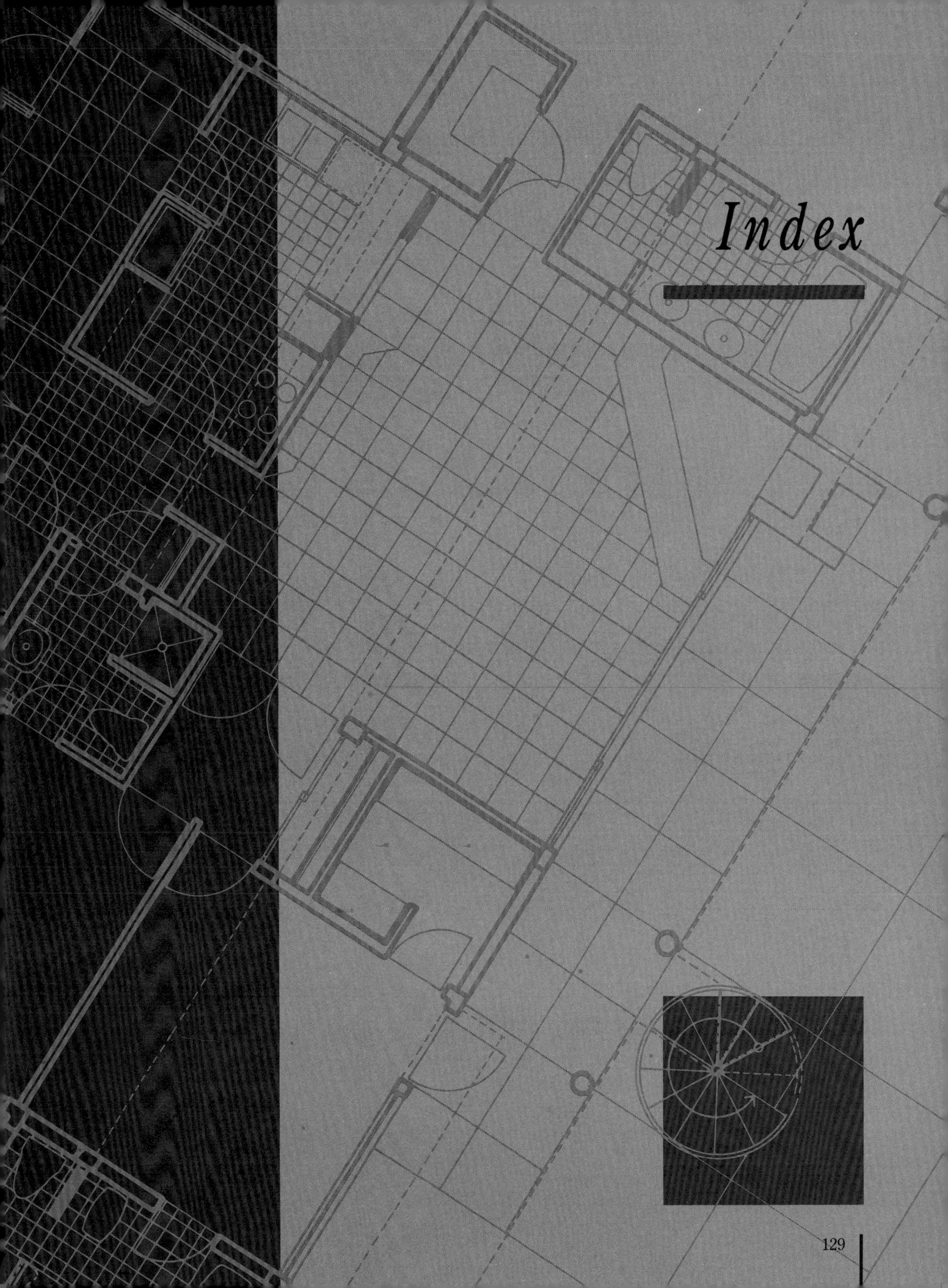

• *Entrant in the American Institute of Architects 1990 Housing Publications review. Others were chosen by the editor to appear in this volume.*

•	Architectural Resources Cambridge, Inc.	18-19
•	The Balsamo/Olson Group, Inc.	90-91
•	Becker/Morgan Architects, Inc.	20-21
	Calthorpe Associates	124-125
•	CBT/Childs Bertman Tseckares & Casendino Inc.	74-77
•	Charlan, Brock & Associates, Inc.	92-93
	Frank Dimster, AIA	36-37
	Downing, Thorpe & James, Inc.	62-63
•	EDI Architecture/Planning	60-61
•	Peter Forbes and Associates, Inc.	22-23
	David Lawrence Gray and Associates, Architects, AIA	38-39
•	House + House	24-27
•	Hugh Newell Jacobsen, FAIA	14-17
		28-29
•	Kanner Architects	94-95
•	Looney Ricks Kiss Architects, Inc.	118-119
•	Donald MacDonald, FAIA	78-81
	Mark Mack	40-41
•	Susan Maxman Architects	30-31
	Muse-Wiedemann Architects	42-43
	John Vaughan Mutlow, AIA	100-101
		102-103

- Kenneth Neumann/Joel Smith and Associates, Inc.   32-33
- John R. Orcutt   114-117
  120-123

  Antoine Predock Architect   44-45

  Rob Wellington Quigley, AIA   106-107

- Rick Rados Architect   34-35
- William Rawn Associates, Architects   82-85
  86-89

- Sasaki Associates, Inc.   114-117
  120-123

- Chris Schmitt & Associates, Inc.   54-55
  56-59

- David M. Schwarz/Architectural Services P.C.   96-97

  Solomon, Inc.   46-47
  64-65

  Robert A.M. Stern Architects   66-67
  126-127

- William F. Stern & Associates, Architects   104-105

  James Wentling/Architects   68-69

  Wenzel & Associates   108-109

- Johannes Van Tilburg & Partners   98-99

  Buzz Yudell   48-49

The information and illustrations in this publication have been prepared and supplied by the entrants. While all reasonable efforts have been made to ensure accuracy, the publishers do not, under any circumstances, accept responsibility for errors, omissions and representations express or implied.